June

BEYOND THE Masquerade

Being Genuine in an Artificial World

NANCY EICHMAN

BEYOND THE *Masquerade*

Being Genuine
in an Artificial World

GOSPEL
ADVOCATE

A TRUSTED NAME SINCE 1855

Also by
Nancy Eichman

Seasoning Your Words

God's Makeover Plan

Keeping Your Balance

Conquering Your Giants

The Road to Forgiveness

Getting Along

Published by Gospel Advocate Co.
1006 Elm Hill Pike, Nashville, TN 37210
www.gospeladvocate.com

ISBN: 978-0-89225-647-1

"Reality ... is found in Christ"

(Colossians 2:17).

To Steve and Dianna Teel –
Your friendship through the years has been an anchor to me.

To Phil Eichman, John Eichman, Phil and Amy White –
Your encouragement puts the wind in my sails.

Table of CONTENTS

Are You Living the
MASQUERADE?

"**S**he's fake."
"She's a phony."
"It's all just an act."

We all know women who put on a facade – a mask – to impress others. Sometimes they are wannabes who pretend to be somebodies. Maybe they are posers who want to look better than they really are. Perhaps they are hiding something, so they "chameleon" their way through life, transforming themselves to fit their surroundings by pleasing others. These women are living the masquerade. They are living in a world of pretense and put-on, where things are not as they seem. They change masks as frequently as they need to. After all, to them it's all a charade.

In this world of designer knockoffs, imitation leather and artificial sweetener, we discover that people can be artificial too. They play one another in the game of life. They lack sincerity and depth and wear plastic smiles. They put up a front while they watch their back. They don't say what they mean or mean what they say.

Ironically, in a world where many of us want 100 percent cotton, pure orange juice, and the genuine article, we suffer from a lack of integrity in relationships. We want the real thing – true love, a genuine friend, and bona fide relationships. Sadly, we are often disappointed with other people. Sometimes we are disappointed with our own lack of authenticity, especially when it comes to our relationship with God. For whatever reasons, we wear masks to hide who we really are, how we really feel, or what we really think. These masks prevent us from being who God wants us to be, and we end up being artificial. We join the masquerade.

But there is hope! As Christian women, we don't have to hide behind any masks in our relationships with others. We have God's Word, which gives us an unmistakably clear picture of One who walked a perfectly genuine life here on earth. While the world turns to virtual reality and artificial intelligence, we can embrace reality, which, as Paul said, "is found in Christ" (Colossians 2:17).

By examining the lives of men and women in the Bible, we can learn what made some people real in their relationship with God and others. We can also learn to avoid the masks others wore and, instead, to develop qualities that will make us authentic. We can learn how to become the genuine women God wants us to be. Are you ready to live beyond the masquerade and share a refreshingly unique and genuine way of life?

Chapter One

Canceling the Show of
PRETENSE

"I don't never have any trouble in regulating my own conduct,
but to keep other folks straight is what bothers me." – Josh Billings

What are other people really like in the privacy of their own homes –
or on a deserted island – or in a restaurant wooing their potential
mate? Someone must have set out to answer those questions when they
created reality TV. Coined "fly-on-the-wall TV," reality TV supposedly
delivers the best and worst of real people to viewers as if they were flies
on the wall. They see ordinary people do wacky, embarrassing, cruel
or even dangerous things we would not usually see or hear.

However, it's ironic that in reality TV producers often manipulate
scripts, fabricate environments and alter the sequence of events to fit
their filming schedule and production standards. As Ray Richmond,
former TV critic for the *Hollywood Reporter*, says: "What they are doing on these shows is taking a kernel of fact and using it to construct
a multi-pronged piece of fiction in the guise of truth and actuality.
This makes for a product that's not only mislabeled but disingenuous
and deceptive." [1]

Do millions of viewers of reality TV know that things are not exactly
as they seem? Do they care? What really seems to matter is that they
are being entertained. The producers are doing whatever it takes to put
on a show. To them, putting on a show is what it's all about.

The Greeks Started It

About 2,000 years ago, the ancient Greeks knew how to put on a show too. Although their productions were different from ours today, they were no less entertaining to the crowds that flooded into the tiers of seats on the hillside theaters to watch the stage below.

An actor would wear a mask made of linen or wood that he could slip on and off easily. The mask's features were exaggerated so the emotions portrayed could be seen to the far seats up in the theater. The actor would come out wearing a smiling mask to say a funny monologue. The audience might roar with laughter as they watched him rushing off to don a frowning mask. He would "answer back" with his solemn lines in the next tragic scene.

This actor was called *hupokrites*, the Greek word meaning "one who answers." Look slightly familiar? It is the word from which we derive our word "hypocrite." This did not start out as a derogatory term, but it evolved from meaning an "actor" to a "pretender" or "one who acts a part, one who wears a mask to cover his true feelings, one who puts on an external show while inwardly his thoughts and feelings are very different." [2]

Understanding the original definition of "hypocrite" makes it easy to see how Jesus in Matthew 23 used that term over and over to describe some of the Pharisees who acted "holier than thou" rather than holy. The term perfectly described these spiritual charlatans who acted out their religious parts in front of the crowds.

Great Performances

The Pharisees put on a great show too! In fact, watching them might have provided some comic relief to the onlookers of Jesus' time. The religious exercises that many in this devout sect underwent daily must have been quite a spectacle. They paraded their righteousness as a grand production for others to see.

For example, picture a grown man walking around bruised and bleeding from bumping into buildings and doorposts. He had a special reason for being battered. His eyes were closed. Why? He didn't want to see any women. No self-respecting orthodox Pharisee would talk to a woman – not even his wife or sister – in public. These devout law-keepers took it a step further and refused to even look at these creatures of such a seemingly low status. Their wounds from bumping into things became their badge of piety!

The Jews called these particular Pharisees "Bruised" or "Bleeding" or "Self-Afflicting Pharisees." This group was one of seven different types the Jews wrote about at a much later date in the Talmud, their book of Jewish traditions. In it, they described the various subgroups of the Pharisees. Six out of seven subgroups were not complimentary.[3]

In all fairness, there were God-fearing Pharisees who truly loved God and wanted to serve Him. The Talmud had good words for this faithful kind of Pharisee, but not the others.

Take for example, the "Hump-Backed" or "Pestle and Mortar Pharisee," also called the "Tumbling Pharisee." These stooped-over men, whose bodies resembled a humpback shape, lowered their gaze and bent over to advertise their humility. The tumbling came from tripping over any obstacle as they scooted along without lifting their feet from the ground. What a ridiculous spectacle they must have made when they shuffled and tumbled along!

Then there was the "Shoulder Pharisee," who observed the Law in meticulous detail but whose good deeds were for show and worn on his shoulder. Or take the "Wait-a-Little Pharisee," who followed the Law but seemed to always think of an excuse for putting off something that needed to be done. There was also the "Ever-Reckoning" or "Compounding Pharisee," who counted up his good deeds as if they were money. The more good deeds he accumulated, the more he felt God was in his debt. Religion was a matter of how much God owed him. The "Timid" or "Fearing Pharisee" was in terror of divine punishment and lived his life in order to escape judgment at all costs.[4]

Just seeing those ridiculous Pharisees – bleeding, tumbling or counting – might have been humorous if it had not been so terribly sad. This sect was bound by its legalism and entrapped by its traditions. Their theatrics did not fool Jesus. He called the teachers of the Law and the Pharisees "blind guides," "blind fools" and "blind men" (Matthew 23:16-17, 19). Jesus had seen enough of their fake religion to level a scathing rebuke at their say-one-thing-and-do-another lifestyles. He succinctly described them: "Everything they do is done for men to see" (v. 5). Their masks of hypocrisy had in turn blinded them.

Their blindness obstructed for them what Jesus could clearly see. The Pharisees, the leading religious leaders of their day, were living the masquerade because they ultimately were living a lie. Who better to lead this masquerade than "the father of lies," the devil (John 8:44)? Paul, in speaking of deceitful characters, penned: "And no wonder, for Satan himself masquerades as an angel of light. It is not surprising, then, if his servants masquerade as servants of righteousness. Their end will be what their actions deserve" (2 Corinthians 11:14-15).

Not the Only Ones

The Pharisees did not have a monopoly on wearing spiritual masks of hypocrisy. There are other examples in the Bible of people who wanted to put on a show to look good before others.

The prophets of the Old Testament railed against the hypocrisy of God's people in putting on a religious show. Isaiah preached against Judah's meaningless oaths in the name of the Lord; their fasting, which had become a mockery; and their "holier than thou" attitudes (Isaiah 48:1-2; 58:3-8; 65:1-5). Jeremiah chastised Judah for claiming to worship God in the temple while they committed murder, theft, adultery and perjury (Jeremiah 7:9-11). Ezekiel condemned the nation of Israel for not practicing what they supposedly believed (Ezekiel 33:31).

In the New Testament, Ananias and Sapphira claimed they had brought all the money they had received from the sale of their property to the apostles, but it was only a portion of the price (Acts 5:1-11). Peter upbraided them for their hypocrisy, and the Lord struck them dead.

Later, Peter himself was described as a hypocrite. In Antioch, Peter initially ate meals with Gentiles but later refused their fellowship when Jewish Christians arrived. Others, including Barnabas, were led astray by his hypocrisy. Paul rebuked Peter to his face in front of the group. Peter was afraid of what his Jewish brothers would think of him instead of doing what he knew was right. In his heart, he knew that Gentile and Jewish Christians had full fellowship with one another, but at the time it seemed more important to impress the Judaizers (Galatians 2:11-14).

No doubt Peter learned a valuable lesson from this encounter in Antioch. Later, he wrote to Christians in Asia Minor, where Jewish and Gentile Christians lived, worked and worshiped together. How were these former enemies to treat one another? He exhorted these fellow Christians to be genuine in their love, not hypocritical. He wrote, "Now that you have purified yourselves by obeying the truth so that you have sincere love for your brothers, love one another deeply, from the heart" (1 Peter 1:22). The Greek term for "sincere" that Peter used meant "without hypocrisy or pretense," but it originally meant "inexperienced in the art of acting." In this particular instance, it was good to be a rookie actor! [5]

What Does It Mean to Be Genuine?

What is this sincerity or genuineness that Peter urged us to strive for? Maybe words like "real," "authentic," "true" and "unaffected" come to mind. To be genuine means to be truly who we are without hiding behind any masks. We speak from the heart. We act with integrity. We express how we think and feel without devaluing the feelings and opinions of others.

However, being genuine is not necessarily doing what comes naturally. It is not raw exposure of our innermost being to everyone. It is not impulsively dumping our "hit and run" reactions on people.

Living an authentic and genuine life means that when we ask someone how she is, we care and really want to know. It means that we look into people's eyes when they talk to us, and we actually listen. It means we try to serve with a sincere desire to help instead of being driven by guilt or compulsion.

We have to admit that sometimes it can be risky to be genuine. It takes courage to act according to our beliefs and defy the crowd. It can be scary to tell how we feel and what we think to others. They might disagree or think we are stupid. They might reject us, argue with us, laugh in our faces, or gossip about us behind our backs.

However, living a sham can be even more difficult. People rarely wear masks for very long without their pretense showing. As American author Nathaniel Hawthorne once wrote, "No one man can, for any considerable time, wear one face to himself, and another to the multitude, without finally getting bewildered as to which is the true one." If we live a lie, eventually others will see that we are just putting on a show, and they could possibly reject us anyway – the very thing we were trying to avoid!

The benefits of being genuine far outweigh the risks. When we stop worrying about what other people think, we can enjoy a new freedom. We can acknowledge the One we are really trying to please. We will learn that being honest does not always damage our relationships with others but often enhances and strengthens them. Other people will feel they can trust us. We will be Christian women of integrity. There will be no disconnect between what we do and say and who we are. We can be true to ourselves and to God. We can cancel the show of pretense and move beyond the masquerade. How liberating that will be!

Reality Check

1. What did the word "hypocrite" originally mean? What does it mean today?

2. How did the Greeks use masks in their productions? What other purpose besides dramatic performances could a theater be used for during New Testament times (Acts 19:28-41)?

3. Why did Jesus describe the Pharisees as hypocrites? What words could describe hypocrites today?

4. Why were the categories of Pharisees in the Talmud described that way?

5. In what ways were some people in the Bible hypocritical?

6. What does it mean to be genuine? What are some specific examples of authenticity in people you have seen?

7. Why is being genuine not necessarily doing what comes naturally?

8. Why is it sometimes risky to be genuine? How can it be more difficult to live behind a mask?

9. What objects are used to describe hypocrisy in these verses: Psalm 55:21; Proverbs 26:23; Matthew 23:27; Luke 12:1? How are these good descriptions of what hypocrisy is like?

10. Do you think Paul was showing off when he listed the ways he had suffered for Christ (2 Corinthians 11:21–12:10)? Why, or why not?

Flash & Flourish

When an upstart actor outshines the star, he "steals the show," and that often described the Pharisees in their dress and daily activities. To call attention to themselves, they wore large leather boxes containing scriptures called "phylacteries," which they attached to their foreheads and left wrists. Broadening these phylacteries could have meant making the straps wider (to show them off more) or wearing them all day instead of just at morning or evening prayer (to show them off longer). The Pharisees wore long tassels on their prayer shawls, for one was considered more pious the longer his tassels were.

The Pharisees' showiness didn't stop with their dress. Jesus told how they loved the best places near the host at a banquet or up front in the synagogues. Greetings were very important in that culture, and it was insulting not to greet a teacher. The Pharisees loved to be greeted with esteemed titles like "Rabbi" in the marketplace, where everyone could appreciate their elevated position. Jesus pointed out that it was the lowly "understudy" (servant) and not the one who steals the show who would ultimately be honored (Matthew 23:5-12).[6]

Chapter Two

Spotting a
FRAUD

"Forgive me for being two-faced. I'm trying to change."
– Unknown

I n the Audrey Hepburn film *How to Steal a Million,* Hepburn's father in the film was a lovable but dishonest art restorer. He restored art so well that he could paint a canvas or create a sculpture to look like an original by adding the right patina to the finish. His finished works fooled the average art buyer as well as the most finicky art connoisseur. By mass-producing these "genuine masterpieces," this imposter became quite rich.

But there's a sad irony about this art fraud. To reproduce artistic masters, he had to be an excellent artist himself. If he had spent his time and energy painting and sculpting under his own name, who knows how well he could have done! Instead, he produced realistic replicas.

Some women are just like that art fraud. They spend their lives masquerading on the outside to cover who they really are on the inside. They work so hard trying to be what someone else thinks they should be that they miss being the original masterpieces they really are. They are religious counterfeits who look like the real thing but under their masks they are spiritual frauds.

Exposing Spiritual Frauds

Jesus knew some spiritual frauds in His day. He could spot them a mile away. He could look into their hearts and know when they were acting one way but thinking another. He zeroed in on the religious leaders, made up primarily of the Pharisees. They tangled almost constantly with Jesus because He exposed them for who they really were.

To be fair, being a member of this Jewish party did not automatically make one a fraud, nor did it make him "Pharisaical." Some Pharisees really tried to live righteous lives. The Jewish masses greatly respected them for their devotion to the Law and their influence in the Sanhedrin. Remember that Paul talked of his life as a Pharisee, not with reproach but as a title of honor.

Their name – Pharisees – meant "separated ones," and that's what they did: separated from sinners, publicans, Gentiles and the "great unwashed" of society. They counted the oral law (the "tradition of the elders" mentioned in Mark 7:3, 5) as equal to the written Law (Torah). So they spent all their lives trying to obey the intricate commands of the Law as well as man-made rules and regulations.[1] They would go to great lengths to follow each detail required of ritual purity in food preparation, ceremonial cleansing and meticulous tithing. In their zeal for righteousness, they took their traditions to seemingly ridiculous extremes, and the letter of the Law became their law. Their righteousness became self-righteousness.

Jesus was a loyal Jew and followed the Law (Mark 1:40-45; 14:12). He acknowledged the authority and validity of the teachings of the Pharisees: "The teachers of the law and the Pharisees sit in Moses' seat. So you must obey them and do everything they tell you" (Matthew 23:2-3).

But then He warned the crowds of their example: "But do not do what they do, for they do not practice what they preach. They tie up heavy loads and put them on men's shoulders, but they themselves are not willing to lift a finger to move them" (Matthew 23: 3-4). The Pharisees tried to follow all those rules and bind them on others while their hearts were rebellious, insincere and hateful. They missed the whole point. They tried to look like masterpieces on the outside when they were only frauds underneath.

John Fischer aptly described the Pharisees' duplicity:

> They set themselves as the holy ones who have the inside
> track on God. ... Like the Wizard of Oz, Pharisees erect a
> god ominous and powerful and bigger than everybody and
> then go behind the facade and control it from the inside so
> as to make themselves its high and lofty representatives and
> the people their spiritual subjects.[2]

Dirty Cups and Rotting Bones

Jesus listed more of the Pharisees' fabrications in Matthew 23 – a
chapter of "woes" and a stinging rebuke of seemingly religious men
who were deep down irreligious. The word "woe" is the opposite of the
word "blessed" in the Beatitudes (5:3-12). "Woe" implies a curse rather
than a blessing. Prophets like Moses used expressions like these as a
form of prayer, having the people repeat "Amen!" after each phrase
(Deuteronomy 27–28). So these "woes" were pretty serious stuff.

One of the "woes" Jesus delivered dealt with the discrepancy between
a person's inside motives and outside actions (Matthew 23:25-28). The
Pharisees were so concerned about purity that they argued about how
clean their cups should be! They washed not only themselves but also
their dishes in ritual baths. At that time, the well-respected rabbi Shammai taught that only the outside of the cup had to be clean, and many
of the Pharisees agreed with him. But those in the school of Hillel,
another rabbi contemporary with Jesus, thought that the inside had to
be cleansed first. Jesus agreed with Hillel, but then took the discussion
to a deeper spiritual level. The Lord taught that the inside of a person
(his heart) needs to be cleansed of the filth of sin before he can really
be clean (pure).[3]

Then Jesus brought up the most dreaded of all sources of unclean-
ness: a corpse. To touch a dead body or a grave made one unclean
for a week (Numbers 19:11, 16). The Pharisees went beyond that and
taught that even if a person's shadow touched a grave or corpse, he was
unclean! To make sure this didn't happen, tombs were whitewashed or
plastered with lime before Passover to warn unsuspecting pilgrims to
avoid this source of contamination. Jesus told the Pharisees that, like

whitewashed tombs, they appeared righteous on the outside, but on the inside they were rotten like a dead man's bones.[+]

Knowing the Real Thing

Just as it takes a real expert to expose an art fraud, it took Jesus to expose the inauthentic Pharisees. Jesus can still spot a fraud, even if we do not always see through one. He knows if we are genuine or not. He knows if we are trying to mask our real motives by righteous-looking actions.

Would Jesus look at us and begin with "Woe to you ..." because of the disparity between what we think and what we do? For example, do we act friendly to visitors at church services but inwardly wish they would go back to the low-income housing where they came from? Do we give our money to help an orphanage while we inwardly wish we could use the money on a new jacket? Do we smile at the elderly lady in front of us who is fumbling to find her money in the grocery checkout lane while we fume impatiently inside? How can we learn to be genuine front to back, inside and out?

When it comes to being genuine, few people know that word's meaning better than the U.S. Department of the Treasury. Workers are specially trained to identify counterfeit money, but they don't spend their time looking at examples of counterfeit bills. Rather, they become so familiar with the genuine bills that they can identify counterfeit bills from the difference in the portrait, seals, border, serial numbers, paper and even the way they feel.

In the same way, the only way we can know how to be authentic children of God is by becoming familiar with the real thing: Jesus. When Jesus said "I am ... the truth" (John 14:6), He affirmed His reality. He shines as our ultimate example of someone who was who He said He was. His motives were pure, and His actions, straightforward. No one was more authentic. He could look into people's souls with genuine concern and touch them physically and spiritually. Let's look at how we can be more like the genuine Jesus – without any masks.

Let the Unmasking Begin

Actively listen. Have you ever tried to talk to someone who was glued to the TV or absorbed in her phone? Have you ever been frustrated when people wouldn't listen to you when you talked to them? You saw them glancing around the room, looking for someone more interesting.

It is much like the Washington diplomat who grew weary of standing in reception lines where no one listened to him. He decided to say something outlandish to see what would happen. He shook hands and began to whisper to each person, "I murdered my mother." Each one in line would smile and say something like "Good job!" or "Isn't that wonderful?" or "Keep up the good work!" Toward the end of the line, a new official came through. When he heard the diplomat's supposed crime, he acted shocked but then recovered by saying, "She probably deserved it."

When we talk with people, we need to focus on them with all our senses and use body language to let them know we care. Paul complimented Timothy for his attentive attitude: "I have no one else like him, who takes a genuine interest in your welfare" (Philippians 2:20). He also gave us the reason why people aren't more attentive: "For everyone looks out for his own interests, not those of Jesus Christ" (v. 21). People are often more concerned about what's going on with themselves than what's going on with anyone else. We need to rise above that mentality and really be there for others.

Forgive fully. Anything we do halfheartedly is in a sense living insincerely and artificially. In this way, if we satisfy ourselves with halfhearted apologies and say, "We'll let it go this time," we miss the freedom that comes through complete forgiveness. It's like the man who said, "I might bury the hatchet, but I will certainly remember where it's buried!" To prevent bitterness from taking root in our hearts, we must fully forgive from the heart. In the parable of the unforgiving servant, Jesus said that's how we must forgive others – from our hearts – because we have been so graciously forgiven by God (Matthew 18:35).

Display your joy. As Christians, we have so many reasons to rejoice. There is no need for artificial smiles because our joy breaks out all over in genuine smiles! Peter gave us the reason for this joy: Jesus. "Though you have not seen him, you love him; and even though you do not see him now, you believe in him and are filled with an inexpressible and glorious joy" (1 Peter 1:8). Peter probably did not smile all the time, but I believe people could see the joy in his face.

Some Christians walk around like Grumpy from the seven dwarfs. They are like the traveler who just arrived at an airport terminal, and some church members asked him if he was their visiting minister. He answered: "No, I'm not the one you're looking for. It's my ulcers that make me look this way!" Like many others in the world, this man believed religion makes people sour and serious. Nothing could be further from the truth! The truly abundant life in Jesus does not make one a grouch, grump or sourpuss. As comedian Joe E. Brown said: "I have no understanding of a long-faced Christian. If God is anything, He must be joy." [5]

Serve wholeheartedly. Wherever we are working – in school, at home, at work, in the church, in the community – we need to do it with all our hearts. Christ's servant attitude needs to flow through us. Paul was referring to slaves in the following passage, but the principle applies to us nevertheless:

> Slaves, obey your earthly masters in everything; and do it, not only when their eye is on you and to win their favor, but with sincerity of heart and reverence for the Lord. Whatever you do, work at it with all your heart, as working for the Lord, not for men, since you know that you will receive an inheritance from the Lord as a reward. It is the Lord Christ you are serving. (Colossians 3:22-24)

No matter where we are, we know that Jesus is ultimately our boss.

A Breath of Fresh Air

Jesus was a breath of fresh air in the stale Pharisaism of His time. He ripped off the fraudulent facades of these religious leaders and challenged His listeners to be genuine and true. The apostle Peter echoed the Lord's message in 1 Peter 2:1. Perhaps flinching from his own failings, he admonished the recipients of his epistle to "rid yourselves of all malice and all deceit, hypocrisy, envy, and slander of every kind." He encouraged them to be genuine, not hypocritical.

In fact, it was the early church's authenticity, among other things, that attracted many believers to the faith. "Every day they continued to meet together in the temple courts. They broke bread in their homes and ate together with glad and *sincere* hearts, praising God and enjoying the favor of all the people" (Acts 2:46-47, emphasis added). The fellowship, joy and praise of these early disciples were genuine manifestations of gratitude for their salvation. This sincerity got the attention of those outside. Outsiders could see this was real. The result? "And the Lord added to their number daily those who were being saved" (v. 47).

Today is no different. If we are to appeal to our artificial world, we must offer something real. Why should they give up what they have if we have nothing better to offer them? There has to be substance in what we say and do. Sooner or later, they will spot a fraud. What will they see in our lives?

Reality Check

1. Why did the Pharisees go to such lengths to follow the Law and tradition in detail? Why did Jesus acknowledge the Pharisees' authority but condemn their example (Matthew 23:2-3)?

2. In Jeremiah 17:5-8, what was the difference between those "cursed" and those "blessed"?

3. How did Shammai differ from Hillel regarding the washing of cups? How did Jesus take the discussion to a deeper spiritual level?

4. How did the Pharisees take the teaching in the Law regarding touching a corpse to the extreme? How did Jesus use their practices to make a point about living behind a facade?

5. How can focusing on the Lord's authenticity help us be genuine? What are some specific examples of His genuine life?

6. What are some ways we can actively listen to people and take a genuine interest in their welfare (Philippians 2:20)?

7. Why is it sometimes difficult to forgive from the heart (Matthew 18:35)?

8. How do you think Paul found true joy in any circumstance (Philippians 4:4)? How can we find true joy today in any circumstance?

9. What are some ways we can be genuine in our daily work? No matter what we do, to whom are we ultimately accountable?

10. What makes a person pharisaical? How can we be pharisaical through our judgment of the Pharisees?

Children *of* Snakes

Like John the Baptist before Him, Jesus spotted the frauds – the teachers of the Law and the Pharisees – and called them a "brood of vipers" (Matthew 23:33). They were that bad, and Jesus said their actions would condemn them to hell.

In Jesus' final "woe" in Matthew 23:29-39, He leveled harsh criticism at their two-sided lives. He accused them of honoring the graves and building elaborate tombs for the prophets when in reality they were the descendants of the very ones who had killed them. In effect, Jesus was saying, "Like father, like son." Their evil lives were not much different than those of their ancestors. Jesus said He would send prophets, wise men and teachers; and these fraudulent leaders would have the chance to repent, but they would not listen.

Jesus' severest rebuke was moderated by His most poignant lament: "O Jerusalem, Jerusalem, you who kill the prophets and stone those sent to you" (Matthew 23:37). The Lord compared Himself to a hen gathering her chicks, but these people were not willing to come to Him. They resisted Jesus' message to the end. Author Brennan Manning stated it well: "Jesus did not die at the hands of muggers, rapists or thugs. He fell into the well-scrubbed hands of deeply religious, totally respectable members of society." [6]

Chapter Three

Dodging the
SNOB MOB

*"Hypocrisy is the essence of snobbery, but all snobbery
is about the problem of belonging." – Alexander Theroux*

Little girls love to form secret clubs with their friends. They might
concoct a secret sign that distinguishes a member of their club
from another or think up elaborate passwords to enter club meetings.
And of course, part of the club mystique is making up membership
rules to follow after a member is "in." Probably the most important is
"No boys allowed!"

As we get older, the rules are different, but we still form clubs,
called "cliques," in which some people are not allowed to join. For
some, getting "in" is very important, but keeping certain people
"out" is even more crucial. These cliques engender snobbery, which
thrives on an affected "I'm better than you" mindset. It doesn't
matter to snobs where they masquerade because there is always
someone to ignore or disdain. Snobbery can be found in various
groups in the neighborhood, in civic groups and in schools – but it
doesn't end there. Even church members sometimes think certain
types of people are just not good enough for their congregations,
and they do all in their power to let them know. Other Christians
have unspoken "requirements" that must be fulfilled before one can
join their group. Unfortunately, snobbery has existed among God's

people for a long time. Let's look at an Old Testament prophet who was a deep down, diehard snob.

"I'm Outta Here!"

When God called Isaiah, he replied: "Here am I. Send me" (Isaiah 6:8). In contrast, when God called Jonah, I imagine that in his mind he answered: "Uh, no way, Lord. Not Nineveh! I'm outta here!" (see Jonah 1:3). Talk about a reluctant prophet!

If Jonah had membership rules in his club, the first would have been "No Ninevites allowed!" Why was Jonah so resistant to the Lord's command to preach to the Ninevites? Why did he find them so distasteful? Did he have a personal vendetta against this wicked city? Or did his national pride against the evil nation of Assyria cause his disdain? Was he afraid to go because of their reputation as annihilating conquerors? Whatever the reason, Jonah caught a ship to Joppa – a city as far away as he could go.

Three days and nights in a big, smelly fish allowed the prophet plenty of time for reflection, and eventually, he changed his mind – at least about going and preaching. After the fish spat him out, he was ready to go to Nineveh.

Or was he? His sermon must have been convincing because all the Ninevites – from the greatest to the least in the kingdom – repented in sackcloth and ashes. They believed God's message through Jonah and declared a fast. God saw that they had turned from their evil ways, and He had compassion on them. He decided not to send the destruction He had threatened, and the Ninevites were saved!

Imagine how Jonah might have felt. When God had first asked him to go and he had gotten over his initial resistance (with a little help from a big fish), he still probably hoped the Lord would bring down destruction on his country's mortal enemy. Just when he could relish God's justice, now Nineveh would remain as a thorn in his country's side – and *he* would be to blame! God had put him in a real predicament. Jonah didn't even like the Ninevites, much less love them. He saw them as bad people who didn't deserve God's grace.

And Jonah ought to have known – about grace, that is. God had just given him a second chance in the belly of the fish, but he thought the Ninevites were not worthy of any second chances. He was all set up for a ringside seat to see Nineveh destroyed, and now the show was canceled. Jonah figured he might as well die. He didn't want to be around when God saved such wicked people. But the Lord is a gracious and compassionate God. Reminding Jonah that Nineveh had a population of more than 120,000 people, God asked Jonah, "Should I not be concerned about that great city?" (Jonah 4:11).

Judging and Labeling

The Lord was displeased with Jonah's high-minded actions and judgmental attitude. Jonah was quick to condemn the Ninevites without giving them a chance. Maybe not by his words, but by his actions Jonah labeled them as "unworthy sinners."

How often do we display prejudice just like Jonah? We shake our heads at his reaction, but are we any better? Do we impose our own membership rules of being "in" or "out" in the church? How many times have you thought or heard:

"She must sleep around – look how she dresses!"

"He's homeless – he must be a drunk!"

"They would have no interest in hearing the gospel – look how they live!"

Do we even bother finding out the truth before thinking or saying such statements? We can develop a nose-stuck-up-in-the-air-looking-down-at-someone-else prejudice about a lot of things when we don't try to understand or find out the truth about what we are seeing. As someone has observed, "Prejudice is being down on something you are not up on." [1] We can judge and exclude people just by their clothes, nationality, race, ethnic background, language, pattern of speech, regional dialect, haircut, religion, place of birth, hometown or section of town – and that isn't all!

Often there are underlying reasons why we judge someone harshly. For example, if we grew up disadvantaged and ridiculed, we may compensate by excluding others and being a snob. Or perhaps we overcame great obstacles to get where we are, and we do not want someone else to take our place. Maybe we had a bad experience with a certain type of person, and we transfer our feelings to others. It may help to look at our past experiences and ask ourselves if we have any unresolved issues that would make us prone to treat others this way.

In the book of James, we read about some in the church having this attitude in worship and why God sees it as wrong. James wrote that exclusivity has no place in the church:

> My brothers, as believers in our glorious Lord Jesus Christ, don't show favoritism. Suppose a man comes into your meeting wearing a gold ring and fine clothes, and a poor man in shabby clothes also comes in. If you show special attention to the man wearing fine clothes and say, "Here's a good seat for you," but say to the poor man, "You stand there" or "Sit on the floor by my feet," have you not discriminated among yourselves and become judges with evil thoughts? (James 2:1-4)

What if God had judged Jacob as a liar or Gideon as a wimp and labeled them unworthy for the tasks He wanted them to do? What if Jesus had not given Zacchaeus the dishonest tax collector or Saul the persecutor a chance? God was able to work in the hearts of these fallen people and make them special in His work. The next time we are tempted to judge and label someone, let's stop and think – what if God had judged and labeled you and me?

The story is told of a lady who accidentally picked up the wrong umbrella belonging to a man in a hotel. The man discovered it, and she was quite embarrassed as she apologetically returned it. The incident reminded her that her daughter and husband needed umbrellas, so she bought some in a nearby shop. As she was leaving with three umbrellas, she ran into the man again, who suspiciously eyed her and said, "You must have had a profitable day after all!" [2]

We are often like the man who judged the "thief." Things might appear different from what they really are. We might not know the whole story. We might not understand people's motives or actions. In the Sermon on the Mount, Jesus said: "Do not judge, or you too will be judged. For in the same way you judge others, you will be judged, and with the measure you use, it will be measured to you" (Matthew 7:1-2). In context, Jesus was referring to judging critically and harshly as the hypocrites did (vv. 3-5). Instead, we are to carefully discern what is right and not judge only by appearances (John 7:24).

Cliques in the Kingdom

It would be nice to think that there are no cliques or snobbery in the church. We hope there would be no hidden membership rules, no secret qualifications for being "in" or "out." Unfortunately, the church is vulnerable to the same judgmental attitudes as the world. The good news is that we have a Savior who can help us overcome these petty attitudes.

Women often feel most keenly the sting of snobbery and exclusiveness in the church. They feel the pressures of fitting in not only for themselves but also for their families. Children and young people can be unkind to the point of cruelty in their disapproval of anyone slightly different than they are.

Women can find themselves ostracized for many different reasons, including their hometown, income or marital status. Sometimes delightful women are excluded simply because they are "not from around here." Some come from a different economic level and can't afford to eat out with others or join them in recreational activities, which for women is often shopping! Singles, divorcees and widows often find it difficult to find a place in churches where couples classes, family seminars and marriage retreats are the only emphasis. Even if the exclusion is not intended, these women still feel it.

If the church does not provide a warm place of genuine love, open acceptance and honest sharing for those who seek a church home, they will seek it elsewhere. They may even reject Christ and His church completely. As Christians, we want to belong to a fellowship of like-minded believers who are joyful and caring. We want to be proud to invite our friends to share this overflowing concern for one another.[3] Cliques have no place in the kingdom of God. As some wise person once said, "Only God is in a position to look down on anyone."

Close Friends = Cliques?

Now does all this mean we should not have close friends? Will these relationships develop into cliques that exclude others?

Do you remember the close relationship between Jesus and three of His disciples (Peter, James and John)? Was their friendship a clique?

Out of the 12 apostles, Jesus asked only these three to join Him at three special times: at the raising of Jairus' daughter, at the Transfiguration, and in the Garden of Gethsemane. The important question is, was their friendship exclusive? We know that Jesus had a wide range of friends including His disciples; Lazarus and his sisters, Martha and Mary; some Pharisees; some women; and some tax collectors. Jesus was open to everyone, so He certainly was not a snob.

It is more likely the Lord called these three out for different reasons. It seemed He was naturally closer to them as friends and depended on their support. For expediency, He could not take all 12 apostles everywhere, but He could take these three in a room to witness a girl raised from the dead, for example. Most important, Peter, James and John were destined to be leaders. Jesus was training them to be "those reputed to be pillars" in the church (Galatians 2:9).

So Jesus had a wide circle of friends, but He also had close friends. Like Jesus, we can be open to everyone but at the same time enjoy friends with whom we feel closer. We just need to be careful not to exclude others or to spend time only with our closest friends, for then we are in danger of forming cliques.

Avoiding the Snob Mob

What then can we do to avoid the "snob mob"?

Be humble. Realize that we are all dependent on the generous grace of God. None of us have any right to put ourselves over anyone else. As Paul reminded us: "Live in harmony with one another. Do not be proud, but be willing to associate with people of low position. Do not be conceited" (Romans 12:16).

See others with compassion. We need to look through eyes of compassion as Jesus did. He touched the untouchable, forgave the unforgivable, and loved the unlovable. When we grow weary of "putting up" with seemingly undesirable people who strain our patience, we need to remember that whenever we serve others, we are really serving Jesus (Matthew 25:40).

Learn to empathize. We need to make a special effort to try to understand the feelings of others. Sometimes people are supersensitive, but at the same time, we can be really insensitive. When we learn to empathize with others' problems, we can see their problems as possibly being our own. At another time in our lives, they just might be (Philippians 2:3-4).

Mix and mingle. Although we love to talk to our friends to find out what is happening in their lives, we need to make an effort to mix and mingle with all kinds of people. We may just learn something! We may be surprised how we can enrich one another's lives and even become really good friends.

Set your radar to people you don't know. In a group, we often gravitate toward those we know. If we always do that, we may miss someone under the "radar screen." Instead, make it a point to introduce yourself to someone with whom you are not familiar. You might just make that person's day!

W.C. Fields once quipped: "I am free of all prejudices. I hate every one equally." [1] For us as Christians, there is a better way! Let's determine to have a "No Excluding Allowed" policy in our lives. Let's ask ourselves: Am I excluding someone unnecessarily or unkindly? Is some prejudice standing in my way? Am I just not thoughtful enough of the feelings of others who want to belong? Am I willing to go the extra mile to make someone feel included? How can I generously and genuinely open my heart to others? Instead of allowing an exclusive club mentality, let's take a stand against any kind of snobbery and cliquishness.

Reality Check

1. What are some possible reasons Jonah was resistant to share God's message to the Ninevites? What was the result of Jonah's preaching?

2. How did God show grace to Jonah and Nineveh? What demonstrated Jonah's real attitude toward the Ninevites?

3. What are cliques, and why are they harmful? How were the Pharisees like a clique?

4. How do past experiences affect how women treat others?

5. What situation did James use as an example of discrimination in worship (James 2:1-4)? What are some ways we discriminate in worship today? Why did James warn against this type of behavior?

6. What was the context of Jesus' command to not judge in Matthew 7:1-2? How are we to judge wisely (John 7:24)?

7. How were these people labeled, and why?
   • John the Baptist and Jesus (Luke 7:33-35).

   • The man born blind (John 9:34).

   • Paul (Acts 28:4-6).

8. Why may women not feel welcome in our fellowship? What are some ways we can be proactive in making sure no one feels excluded in our church activities?

9. Why do you think Jesus chose Peter, James and John to join Him on special occasions? Do you think they were a clique within the apostles? How do we prevent our close friendships from becoming a clique?

10. In a larger group, why is it more difficult to meet others? What can we do to make meeting and greeting others easier and more personal?

The Club
Mentality

~

In or out? You were either "in" with the Pharisees (righteous in their eyes) or totally "out" (sinners). In their kind of spiritual club, they were masters at pigeonholing people and knew just where to put everyone in the religious hierarchy of life.

They thought "ordinary" Jews, whom they called "people of the land," lacked the commitment and knowledge to follow each precept of the Law. They saw themselves as orthodox standard bearers of the truth with the right to judge other teachers like John the Baptist and Jesus (Matthew 3:1-12; 9:1-13). This haughty attitude was evident when the temple guards sent to arrest Jesus returned empty-handed. The guards saw that the Lord, unlike other teachers, taught with authority. In reply, the Pharisees retorted: "Has any of the rulers or of the Pharisees believed in him? No! But this mob that knows nothing of the law – there is a curse on them" (John 7:48–49).

Jesus spoke of the Pharisees' spiritual snobbery when He exclaimed, "You shut the kingdom of heaven in men's faces" (Matthew 23:13). By their strict rules and regulations, they were keeping out those who might want to enter the kingdom. By keeping others out, they themselves would not enter in as well.

Chapter Four

Taught by Jerri Simpson

Sidestepping the
PEOPLE-PLEASING
Trap

*"I know I'm in the rip current of people-pleasing
when I dread saying yes but feel powerless to say no." – Lysa Terkeurst*

They go up. They go down. Public opinion polls ride the waves of current thought. They take the pulse of the people and translate it into percentage points. Whether the poll is taken regarding a product or politician, we get a sense of what people are thinking and how they are feeling. Of course, it depends on who is doing the talking.

As one anonymous wit has quipped: "You can't always go by expert opinion. A turkey, if you ask a turkey, should be stuffed with grasshoppers, grit and worms!" [1]

But how much weight should public opinion polls carry in moral issues? Should they sway those in authority to change policy where right and wrong are concerned? What if public opinion upholds evil in our society? Do high approval ratings mean that someone or something is always worthy of our trust? Pleasing *any* of the people *any* of the time should be open to question.

God's people are called to please Him, not necessarily win public opinion polls. But many people of God find themselves acting totally contrary to what they ought to do. Instead of following the will of God, they succumb to the will of others. Falling into the trap of people-pleasing causes people to change how they talk and how they act, leading to a life of pretentiousness. Let's look at a vivid example of one whose desire to please people led to disastrous consequences.

The Leader Who Was Led

If Moses had been the subject of a public opinion poll in the Israelite camp, he probably would have received spiraling approval ratings. In Exodus 32, the Israelite leader was on Mount Sinai receiving the Law from God. After about 40 days with no word from their leader, the Israelites grew restless and wondered what had happened to him. Aaron, Moses' brother, was caught in a people-pleasing dilemma. He and Hur were left in charge of the children of Israel (24:14). An impatient mob gathered around Aaron and demanded that he provide them some alternate gods to lead them out of the desert.

It seemed not to matter to the people that just before Moses left, God had demonstrated His glory on Mount Sinai to them. The Israelites had witnessed the lightning and thick smoke, heard the deafening thunder and trumpet blast, and experienced the whole mountain trembling violently (Exodus 19:16-19). God commanded Moses to put limits around Mount Sinai because the people would perish if they touched it (v. 12). It was like it had gigantic "No Trespassing" signs all around it because it was holy.

We can understand why. Mount Sinai, also known as the "mountain of God" or Mount Horeb, held special significance to Moses and Aaron in their calling to lead the people out of bondage. It was there that Moses first encountered God in the burning bush (Exodus 3:1-2) and there that Aaron joined his brother and accepted his God-given role to be the spokesman for the two in front of Pharaoh (4:27). It was also there that Moses and Aaron – as well as Aaron's sons, Nadab and Abihu, and the 70 elders of Israel – worshiped God at a distance "and saw the God of Israel. Under his feet was something like a pavement made of sapphire, clear as the sky itself. But God did not raise his hands against these leaders of the Israelites; they saw God, and they ate and drank" (Exodus 24:9-11).

Even if you had only seen the feet of God, would you have felt the need to make an idol to a false god? We would expect that Aaron would have adamantly refused any request to make a false god when he had seen God Almighty! But under pressure, a people-pleaser weakens, and that is just what Aaron did. He told the people to literally "tear off" their earrings – maybe because he was angry with them or with himself for giving in.[2] Perhaps he thought they would refuse to give up their prized booty from the Egyptians (Exodus 12:36). Nevertheless, he took their earrings and fashioned a calf, probably a young bull that symbolized divine power like those found in the pagan religions around them.[3] Then Aaron announced, "These are your gods" (32:4) – a blatant violation of the second command Moses had received from the Lord on the mountain just a few days earlier (20:4-6).

Perhaps to salve his conscience, Aaron combined the worship of God with the calf by building an altar in front of the calf and then holding a festival to the Lord. After this syncretistic attempt to honor God with offerings, the people turned to drunkenness and sexual immorality prevalent in pagan worship at that time.[1] Much like an unprepared substitute teacher, Aaron had been left in charge of a group of unruly "children," and he had let them get out of hand. "Moses saw that the people were running wild and that Aaron had let them get out of control and so become a laughingstock to their enemies" (Exodus 32:25). Although the people were at fault, Moses laid the blame on Aaron as well: "He said to Aaron, 'What did these people do to you, that you led them into such great sin?' " (v. 21).

God grew furious at the revelry below and threatened to build a new nation through Moses and destroy the Israelites then and there! Moses petitioned God for mercy on behalf of the Israelites, especially for his brother, Aaron (Deuteronomy 9:20). God commanded the Levites to kill those who were guilty, and they struck down 3,000 people (Exodus 32:28). Later, the Lord struck the people with a plague (v. 35). What a sad end for many of the people of God!

Profile of a People-Pleaser

As the appointed high priest and spiritual leader of Israel, Aaron failed miserably. He allowed himself to be pressured and manipulated by the people. Aaron's reaction is a classic characteristic of people-pleasers today. Let's look at some of the ways Aaron fit the people-pleaser profile so we can determine whether we might be people-pleasers too.

The Conflict Avoider

Aaron tried to smooth over Moses' anger and avoid more conflict by urging Moses, "Do not be angry, my lord" (Exodus 32:22). After all, Moses was so mad that he broke the tablets of God's Law, ground the golden calf into fine dust, and scattered the dust in the people's drinking water.

Like Aaron, the Conflict Avoider feels pressured to avoid any negative situations or feelings. But she needs to understand that conflict does not always result in open confrontation or fighting. She needs to learn that conflict can be resolved constructively by dealing with it rather than by suppressing it.[5]

The Fixer

Aaron told Moses how the people had urged him to make them gods because their leader had been gone so long. He felt pressured to fix the people's problem quickly in order to make them happy. He thought if he gave them what they wanted, they would be content.

This is the classic move of the Fixer, who tries to work out everyone's problems. This sometimes means she has to go to uncomfortable extremes or do things she might not ordinarily do to find a short-term solution. However, she finds that some problems don't have a quick fix and that, in trying to solve other peoples' problems, she has made more problems for them – and herself.

The Justifier

Aaron tried to justify his behavior by more excuses. He told Moses, "Then they gave me the gold, and I threw it into the fire, and out came this calf!" (Exodus 32:24). He felt pressured to do what he knew he should not do. He knew it was wrong, yet he wanted to please the people.

The Justifier sometimes does things that are wrong to get the approval of others. She feels a compulsion to do whatever it takes to make others happy and make up excuses for her actions. In her mind, the end justifies the means.

Whether they are 16 or 60, some people never outgrow peer pressure, and no matter their age, people-pleasers can really get into trouble. They are like the chameleon that changed his colors to match his surroundings. When he was on a green limb, he would turn green. When he was on a brown tree trunk, he would turn brown. The problem came when he jumped on a Scotch plaid sport coat. He had a nervous breakdown trying to relate to everything at once![6]

From People-Pleaser to God-Pleaser

So what kinds of changes do we need to make in order to stop being people-pleasers?

Please God first. Although we like to please others, especially those we love, it is more important to please God. When we have a heart that strives to please God first, then pleasing people won't be so important. This is how Paul felt: "We are not trying to please men but God, who tests our hearts. ... We were not looking for praise from men, not from you or anyone else" (1 Thessalonians 2:4, 6). In the face of persecution from Jewish leaders, Peter proclaimed, "We must obey God rather than men!" (Acts 5:29).

Deal with conflict. It can be beneficial, even healthy, to deal with conflict in the right way. Using techniques of constructive conflict – such as remaining calm, focusing on the issue at hand, and actively listening to the person talking – can often help us find resolution. Sometimes we can just agree to disagree. But if we avoid facing our differences just to get along, it can backfire. If we always avoid saying how we really think or feel, it can have the opposite effect. Those we want to please could be provoked to frustration, then to anger, and finally to conflict – the very things we wanted to avoid!

Just say no. Saying no can be one of the hardest things we can do. It can make us feel uncomfortable, even guilty. But it is healthy to set boundaries in our lives. When we have limited time and energy, we can find ourselves too close to the breaking point of self-control and patience. It's like someone stepping on our toes. If we warn the offender as soon as it happens, we will save them embarrassment and our toes. But if we wait too long, we might lash out in an angry tirade and have black and blue toes as well![7]

Buy time to make decisions. Often we are rushed or pressured into a decision that we did not want to make. Whether the decision was just inconvenient or seriously immoral, it makes us feel bad afterward, and then we feel guilty about feeling bad! We need to stop automatically saying yes whenever we are asked. Remember Jesus did not always answer questions right away and sometimes not at all (Mark 14:61-62; John 8:6-7).

Perhaps your boss and co-workers are putting pressure on you to go out with them after work and you are unsure about what they might have in mind. You are caught off guard and don't know how to respond. You can delay your answer by saying: "I'm not sure I can make it. Let me get back with you on that." Or a good friend flatters you, praising your decorated cupcakes and asking if you could decorate some for her son's birthday. Instead of giving an answer immediately, you can say: "I don't know if I'll have time to do a good job on that. Let me think about it, and then let you know." After you have time to consider people's requests, you can give them an answer. Buying time will help you weigh your options before you commit to anything.

Escaping the People-Pleasing Quagmire

Why are we so easily sucked into the people-pleasing quagmire? Often we think we should always do what others need, want or expect. By pleasing others, we think others will like, respect and appreciate us. But unfortunately, sometimes people will be unkind to us even if we are kind to them. We might even try harder to be nice, thinking that it will win them over. After a while, we realize it is not our fault. It is their problem. People-pleasing is often a self-defeating cycle that can only be broken by realizing we have no control over others, only ourselves. We would *prefer* that others accept, not reject us. But the fact is not everyone will like us.[8]

We don't have to fall into the trap of people-pleasing, because our self-worth does not depend on what we do for others or whether they like us. In fact, letting others know how we feel and think does not have to diminish our value in their eyes; it might even enhance how they see us when we stand up for ourselves. But ultimately God is the One who truly gives us our worth. Only through His love can we find the freedom to love others and ourselves. Only then can we find freedom from peer pressure and escape the people-pleasing quagmire.

Reality Check

1. What is the danger of allowing public opinion to sway moral issues and public policy? What are some examples in our current culture of this happening?

2. How had God demonstrated His glory just before Moses left to go on Mount Sinai? What significance did Mount Sinai have for Moses and Aaron?

3. Why did the children of Israel grow restless at Mount Sinai when Aaron was left in charge? What was the result of Aaron's people-pleasing?

4. How did Aaron's actions fit the people-pleaser profile? What are some ways we might exhibit these characteristics today?

5. Which other people-pleasing leaders committed evil by succumbing to the clamoring of other people (1 Samuel 15:24; Mark 6:22-28; 15:15; Acts 12:1-4)?

6. How can people-pleasing often backfire?

7. Why is it sometimes difficult to tell people no? What are the benefits of setting physical and emotional boundaries with people?

8. How can dealing with conflict be healthy? What are some techniques of constructive conflict we can adopt?

9. Why is it wise to buy time when making decisions?

10. What is often the real reason we try to win the approval of others? What realization about our self-worth can help us?

Praise-Loving People-Pleasers

The Pharisees could be pretty intimidating. They threatened anyone who acknowledged Jesus as the Christ with being thrown out of the synagogue (John 9:22). For a Jew, it would be a terrible loss to forfeit one's place within the community and family and be excluded from the religious center of Jewish life.

The Pharisee's threat of excommunication was enough to cause some of the Jewish leaders who believed in Christ to be unwilling to openly confess Him. They feared expulsion from the synagogue and the shame and reproach that would bring, "for they loved praise from men more than praise from God" (John 12:43). Earlier in John 5:44, Jesus had upbraided the Jews for their lack of faith: "How can you believe if you accept praise from one another, yet make no effort to obtain the praise that comes from the only God?"

When the Jewish leaders tried to be secret disciples with a pseudo-faith in Christ, their double allegiance could not exist forever. They longed for the approval of men over the approval of God. As the commentator William Barclay observed, "Either the secrecy kills the discipleship, or the discipleship kills the secrecy." [9]

Chapter Five

Taught by
Louise Fowler

Avoiding Games
OF DECEIT

*"Nothing is more common on earth
than to deceive and be deceived." – Johann G. Seume*

G ames of deceit have been played for a long time. Yet they are still as current as the headlines. Whether it is a global manufacturing corporation chairman embezzling millions of dollars, sixth-graders pirating films and music from the Internet, or an acclaimed historian plagiarizing another writer, people are still playing games of deceit.

The word "deceive" has a complex set of meanings. It implies deliberately leading someone into danger, error or misfortune through underhanded or dishonest methods. So whether you trick, betray, beguile, mislead, delude, double-cross, hoodwink or bamboozle, someone is being deceived.

"Why have you deceived me [or us]?" is a common complaint running throughout the pages of the Bible. Jacob asked Laban this question when he ended up with Leah instead of Rachel in his marriage bed the morning after their wedding (Genesis 29:25). Joshua learned the painful truth of the Gibeonites' deception of the Israelites after they made the treaty (Joshua 9:22). The witch of Endor feared punishment from Saul, the king of Israel, when she realized he had deceived her (1 Samuel 28:12).

Even people of God can play games of deceit. Let's look at two people who deceived each other with tragic results.

The Deadly Daughter-in-Law?

Perhaps Jacob's son Judah was superstitious. Judah's first son, Er, had been married to Tamar and then died suddenly. The same thing happened to his second son, Onan. So Judah did not want to risk losing his third and only living son, Shelah, as well. He might have wondered if there was a connection. Then again, those sons had been evil, and the Lord had put them to death (Genesis 38:7, 10).

The Bible specifically states that Onan refused to fulfill his leviratic marriage duty to Tamar, as Judah had asked of him. This duty required the younger son to take the widow of the older son to carry on the bloodline of the family. But Onan knew that any children from their union would not be his but his brother's. Not only would his brother's name be passed on to the child but also his inheritance share. Onan was not willing to share the inheritance with those children, and God was not pleased with his attitude, so He put him to death.

After his first two sons had died, Judah told Tamar to go home. This was not the custom at that time. According to the Law of Moses, only a priest's daughter could honorably go back home to her father's house after she was widowed (Leviticus 22:13). Judah told her to go live in her father's house until Shelah could grow up and then marry her. But Judah had a deceitful plan in mind. He didn't plan to give Shelah to Tamar, at least not soon. He thought he could conveniently forget Tamar – out of sight, out of mind.

But Tamar did not forget. Scripture says "after a long time" Judah's wife died (Genesis 38:12). This seemed to have been enough time for Shelah to grow up. Tamar waited, and still Judah did not call for her. She decided to take action herself.

She took off her widow's garments and wore the veil of a prostitute. As ~~Jacob~~ Judah walked along the road to Timnah to shear his sheep, he asked to sleep with her and offered her a young goat from his flock as payment. Tamar asked for a pledge – a guarantee that he would indeed pay her. He gave her his seal, cord and staff. These were very personal items that would identify him with no question. The seal, which might have been a cylinder or a stamp, was rolled on a clay tablet or pressed into wax as a distinctive way to sign a document. The walking staff probably was unique as well, perhaps being carved and polished.

The Game Plan Backfires

Tamar became pregnant from their encounter and returned to her father's house. When Judah had his friend take one of his goats to the woman he met along the road, she was nowhere to be found.

Tamar kept her secret from him for three months. Then Judah was told of her pregnancy with the news that she was "guilty of prostitution." Judah, not wanting this evil stain on his family name, demanded that she be burned to death. Ironically, this extreme punishment was prescribed only for daughters of priests involved in harlotry and incest, the very sin Judah had engaged in himself (Leviticus 21:9).[1]

As she was being brought out for her punishment, she sent a message to her father-in-law that she was pregnant by the one who gave her the seal, cord and staff. Then the impact of his deceit – and hers – fully hit him. He was the father of her child!

As we look at the deceit of Tamar and Judah and other examples in God's Word, we can see how deceit leads to more deceit, and trickery leads to more trickery. They proved that trickery got them nowhere! Tamar's plan backfired. She was able to have two children, but it is probable from the context that she never married again or had any more children (Genesis 38:26). Judah's plan backfired as well because he certainly could never forget Tamar now that she had born his children. Their grandfather was in fact their father!

The sad truth about this story is that Tamar had a legal recourse through the Law of Moses to call her father-in-law to task. She did not have to become a harlot to get him to act. If Shelah was not going to marry her, Tamar could have gone to the elders at the town gate and told them her husband's brother refused to carry on his brother's name. If he persisted in refusing, she could have gone up to him, taken one of his sandals, and spit in his face. His disgrace would have been that of having a family known as "The Family of the Unsandaled" (Deuteronomy 25:5-10). The guilt would have been on him, not on her.

Weaving the Web of Deceit

Deceit is almost as old as time, beginning when the devil first tricked Eve in the Garden of Eden (Genesis 3:13; 2 Corinthians 11:3). Since then, people have been deceiving others for their own purposes. What are some reasons why deceivers in the Bible wove their own individual webs of deceit?

To Take Advantage

Jacob's sons told the Shechemites to be circumcised so they could marry into their families. Their real purpose was to put the Shechemites in a compromised position so they could be easily attacked and killed. That's exactly what Reuben and Simeon did to avenge their sister Diana's rape at the hands of the prince of Shechem (Genesis 34:13-31).

To Get Something

When the prophet Elijah healed the well-to-do Naaman of his leprosy, Naaman offered him gifts, but Elijah refused. Elijah's servant Gehazi, however, decided he would get something for himself. He ran after Naaman and deceived him into thinking that Elisha had two guests from the company of the prophets. He asked for a talent of silver and two sets of clothing, and Naaman generously gave him more. When Gehazi hid his bounty and returned to Elisha, it was Gehazi who was afflicted with leprosy for the rest of his life (2 Kings 5).

To Retrieve Information

King Herod was bent on destroying the infant King of the Jews – no matter what it took. He secretly called in the wise men and asked them to let him know when they found the baby in Bethlehem so he could go and worship Him too. His real design was to find the child and murder Him. When the wise men did not return, Herod ordered all babies 2 years old and under to be killed so that the infant would not survive (Matthew 2:7-8, 16-18).

To Lead Astray

Jesus warned that false prophets would come in His name and claim, "I am the Christ" and "The time is near," deceiving many and leading Christians away from the truth (Matthew 24:4-5; Luke 21:8). Paul reiterated this when he spoke of a kind of evil masquerade party: "For such men are false apostles, deceitful workmen, masquerading as apostles of Christ. And no wonder, for Satan himself masquerades as an angel of light. It is not surprising, then, if his servants masquerade as servants of righteousness. Their end will be what their actions deserve" (2 Corinthians 11:13-15).

Watch Out!

Jesus warned us, "Watch out that no one deceives you" (Mark 13:5). That is a real challenge in our society. For many people today, deception is a way of life. They tell lies without a second thought. These lies range from misleading half-truths to intentional exaggerations to flat-out untruths. People also deceive by what they do not say, for example in nonverbal cues or even by the subtle spin they put on their words.

So how do we avoid getting bamboozled? Just like the games they play, deceivers come in all shapes and sizes. The Bible warns us of some of their particular ploys. Watch out!

Smooth (In Reality, Trouble)

Be wary of the smooth-talking co-worker or neighbor who causes trouble behind your back. King David aptly described the trouble-making deceiver who has a way with words: "His speech is smooth as butter, yet war is in his heart; his words are more soothing than oil, yet they are drawn swords" (Psalm 55:21).

God-Led (In Reality, Controlling)

Guard against seemingly godly leaders who sway people with their controlling personalities. Paul warned of the "wormers": "… having a form of godliness but denying its power. Have nothing to do with them. They are the kind who worm their way into homes and gain control over weak-willed women, who are loaded down with sins and are swayed by all kinds of evil desires" (2 Timothy 3:5-6).

Rich (In Reality, Poor)

Be aware of "high-on-the-hog" folks who charge their credit cards to the limit to feign a higher standard of living when they keep digging themselves deeper in debt. Solomon wrote, "Better to be a nobody and yet have a servant than pretend to be somebody and have no food" (Proverbs 12:9).

Good (In Reality, Evil)

How many women have dated men who seemed too good to be true only to discover their mates were entirely different after marriage? If you are considering marriage, take time to get to know your prospective mate well before you commit your life to him. Ask others what they think of your fiance. Although ultimately it is your decision, if those you trust think your husband-to-be is a scoundrel, think twice before you marry him. "Though his speech is charming, do not believe him, for seven abominations fill his heart. ... A lying tongue hates those it hurts, and a flattering mouth works ruin" (Proverbs 26:25, 28).

Sympathetic (In Reality, Self-Serving)

Let friendships evolve and pass the test of time. Sometimes we are so excited to find someone who seems to really understand and care about us that we rush to share confidences too soon. After those confidences are shared to the world, we sadly discover our supposed friend was actually a gossip who only cared about getting people's attention with the next big thing. Jeremiah warned that not every friend is genuine (Jeremiah 9:4-6).

Honest (In Reality, Cheating)

Shysters and schemers abound, and we need to check them out to be sure they are reputable. We need to exhibit the animal-like instincts Jesus encouraged in His disciples: "Therefore be as shrewd as snakes and innocent as doves" (Matthew 10:16)

"You destroy those who tell lies; bloodthirsty and deceitful men the LORD abhors" (Psalm 5:6). God hates deceit, and we can understand why. It is a dangerous business when we deal deceitfully. Someone is bound to get hurt. Proverbs 26:18-19 expresses it well: "Like a mad-man shooting firebrands or deadly arrows is a man who deceives his neighbor and says, 'I was only joking!' "

Deceiving Ourselves

We look at the problems that resulted from trickery in the Bible and wonder how they could get in such a mess! But we are not immune to deceiving others. We can even deceive ourselves and not realize it. Some people in the Bible deceived themselves first and then went on to deceive others. Their self-deception resulted in their downfall. Let's look at some self-deceptive thinking that women can still use today.

"Since I'm a good person, I can get away with this if nobody sees me."

King David, the man after God's own heart, really had to deceive himself before he tricked Uriah, orchestrated Uriah's murder, and married the beautiful Bathsheba (2 Samuel 11). The apostle John described this kind of deception: "If we claim to be without sin, we deceive ourselves and the truth is not in us" (1 John 1:8).

"No matter what, God wants me to be happy."

Before David's firstborn son deceived his half-sister Tamar, Amnon deceived himself into thinking his passion for her was love when it was merely lust (2 Samuel 13:1-22). Paul wrote of devious men like Amnon: "Evil men and imposters will go from bad to worse, deceiving and being deceived" (2 Timothy 3:13).

"I'm popular, good-looking and resourceful, so I can do what I want."

The handsome Absalom, another son of David, deluded himself into thinking he could justify murdering his brother Amnon, beguiling the people of Israel, and rebelling against his father (2 Samuel 13:23–18:33). Paul also wrote about this chicanery: "If anyone thinks he is something when he is nothing, he deceives himself" (Galatians 6:3).

A clandestine affair, an underhanded transaction, a hidden sinful pleasure – these evils often start with self-deception. We first delude ourselves into thinking that our sin is acceptable. Do we "fudge" a little on our income tax to get a bigger return? Have we ever given the impression we had more education or experience than we really had in order to get a job? Have we ever misled someone to protect our friends or family? Have we ever been dishonest in taking advantage of a sale item at the store? Even in seemingly small things, we need to avoid trying to fool others. We will never ultimately win any games of deceit.

Reality Check

1. Why did God put Er and Onan to death? Why might Onan have refused to fulfill his leviratic marriage obligation?

2. Why do you think Judah told Tamar to go back to her father's house? According to the Mosaic Law, who could honorably go back to her father's home after she was widowed (Leviticus 22:13)?

3. Why did Judah not recognize Tamar by the road? What was the

pledge that Tamar asked from Judah, and why did she ask for this?

4. Why did Judah demand Tamar be burned to death? What was Tamar's legal recourse that could have avoided deceit?

5. What other women in the Bible thought their only recourse was incest? What resulted from their deceitful plan (Genesis 19:30-38)?

6. Who deceived his father and was later deceived by his sons? What role did clothes play in both these deceptions (Genesis 27:15; 37:31-35)?

7. How can a woman's charm be deceptive today (Proverbs 31:30)?

8. How did Jesus identify Satan in John 8:44? Who called Jesus a deceiver, and why (Matthew 27:63)?

9. What are some ways we might deceive ourselves (James 1:22-26; 1 John 1:8; Galatians 6:3)?

10. What are some kinds of deceit warned against in the Bible? What are some examples of these occurring today?

A Trap
Laid With Taxes

~

The Pharisees and Herodians were unlikely collaborators, but their goal was singular: to trap Jesus with a deceitful question. It is easy to see how the topic of taxes could jump-start controversy and spring a trap at the same time. Taxes were especially unpopular in Palestine because they were a constant reminder of the Romans – the Jews' hated conquerors. After obvious flattery, the tricksters asked Jesus if they should pay the tax. They figured that if He said no, they could accuse Him of treason, and if He said yes, He would lose His followers among the people.

Requesting a Roman coin, Jesus then asked them whose image was on it. They replied, "Caesar's," who at that time was Emperor Tiberius. Jesus turned the tables on them and answered them simply yet profoundly: "Give to Caesar what is Caesar's, and to God what is God's" (Matthew 22:21). In condoning the payment of taxes, Jesus was teaching that God's people should fulfill their obligations. The finagling Pharisees planned to snare Jesus in their trap of deceit. Instead, He escaped so skillfully that they were left empty-handed and amazed (v. 22).

Chapter Six

Rattling Skeletons
IN YOUR CLOSET

"There is a skeleton in every house." – Anonymous

Jim returned home late from work as his wife, Julie, was checking on their 2-year-old son asleep in bed. She came down the stairs to see Jim staring in disbelief at the computer screen she had been viewing. After seeing several pictures of erotic sex on the screen, he looked at Julie's shocked face and asked: "Why didn't you tell me you were into porn? We could have worked together to get some help."

Julie started crying and murmured: "I was so ashamed. I didn't want you to know. I thought I could quit. I just thought it would be better to keep it a secret."

It is not always better to keep things a secret. This family was almost torn apart by the secret Julie refused to talk about and acknowledge. She didn't want to rattle that skeleton in her closet.

Should You Keep a Secret?

Every family seems to have some skeletons in their closets that they don't like to face. Perhaps there is an alcoholic aunt, a gambling father, or an abusive mate that no one wants to acknowledge. A problem arises when secrets keep families from communicating and being real with one another. Holding on to family secrets without working through them can mask the truth and project a lie. It can keep individuals entangled in a web of deceit, shame and anger. It can break trust and breed confusion. It can cause people to deny and repress their feelings. Defense mechanisms take the place of emotions. A facade of being okay is formed to make everything seem all right when it really isn't.

Not all secrets are bad. Nothing is wrong with secrets like surprise parties, rendezvous dates with mates, and weekend getaways with the family. We could use more secrets like those! Jesus taught that when possible, our good deeds should be done in secret so we are not dependent on the praise of others (Matthew 6:1-6). Sometimes God's people used secrecy to protect their lives. The Israelite spies sent to Jericho made a secret oath with Rahab for their mutual escape (Joshua 2:14-21). When David fled from Jerusalem, his spies were secretly hidden in a well by a woman in Bahurim (2 Samuel 17:17-22). Nehemiah inspected the walls of Jerusalem in the secrecy of night (Nehemiah 2:11-16). The early Christians helped Paul escape through an opening in the Jerusalem wall in a basket at night in order to save his life (Acts 9:23-25). Even Jesus acted secretly when necessary (John 7:1-13).

We also might need to use secrecy in certain circumstances as a matter of discretion. Some family matters should be kept confidential for the healing of those involved. Not everyone needs to know our family problems. In cases like these, confidentiality can strengthen and protect the family.

However, hiding a problem to the point of not dealing with it creates an even bigger problem for a family. Let's look at a family in the Bible that kept secrets that grew more damaging with time.

Generational Damage of Family Secrets

Abram was worried. He knew that men would be attracted to his beautiful wife, Sarai, and he was afraid they would kill him to marry her. So he disguised the fact that she was his wife. On two different occasions, two kings – the Egyptian pharaoh and Abimelech, king of Gerar – took who they thought was Abram's sister into their palaces. God intervened in each case with the secret being exposed and Sarai returning to Abram (Genesis 12:10-20; 20).

But the secrets did not stop there. Did Abram, later renamed Abraham, share his almost disastrous escapades with these two rulers with his son Isaac? Or did Isaac not learn from his father's mistakes? Isaac kept the same secret about his wife, Rebekah – again, out of fear – because she too was beautiful. Another Abimelech, king of the Philistines, discovered the truth as he looked from a window and saw Isaac caressing his wife. Abimelech chastised Isaac for his lie and expressed relief that no man had tried to marry her, which would have brought guilt upon him (Genesis 26:1-11).

There were more secrets to come in this family. Later, Isaac and Rebekah each had favorites between their grown twin sons. Rebekah plotted with her favorite son, Jacob, to keep his identity a secret from his nearly blind father, Isaac. Their scheme worked, enabling Jacob to receive his older brother Esau's birthright. When Esau returned, he vowed revenge and planned to kill Jacob. Rebekah overhead his threat and warned Jacob (Genesis 27).

Jacob fled to his Uncle Laban's house, where the secrets continued. Laban surprised Jacob with a real secret on the day of his wedding – he gave him Leah, the wrong sister! Later, Jacob married his beloved Rachel, but as time went on, he grew weary of Laban's trickery in changing his wages 10 times. He secretly fled with his family without telling his father-in-law. Meanwhile, Rachel had stolen Laban's household gods, but as far as we know, he never discovered that secret (Genesis 29:15-30; 31).

The secrets kept coming. Jacob had 12 sons, but because 10 of them grew tired of their brother Joseph's grandiose dreams, they secretly sold him into slavery, saying that a wild beast had killed him. For years, their father carried the grief of their actions, and they carried the guilt of their lie. Years later, the truth was finally exposed in Egypt as Joseph, now second to Pharaoh, forgave them and asked Pharaoh to allow them to live in Goshen (Genesis 37, 45–46).

Several generations later, this family was still keeping secrets. King David's lust resulted in an illicit love affair with Bathsheba. When Bathsheba became pregnant, David secretly planned her husband Uriah's death and had it carried out. Nathan told David his secret would be exposed and would bring calamity to his family: "You did it in secret, but I will do this thing in broad daylight before all Israel" (2 Samuel 12:12).

This prophecy was fulfilled when all kinds of intrigues disrupted David's royal family. David's son Amnon had a secret crush on his half-sister Tamar, which drove him to rape her. Another son, Absalom, held a smoldering but hidden hatred against half-brother Amnon for raping Tamar. That prompted him to kill Amnon. Then Absalom's surreptitious takeover of the people's allegiance culminated in a full-fledged rebellion against his father and, ultimately, in Absalom's tragic death (2 Samuel 13–18).

We can see the heartbreaking effect these secrets had on generation after generation. Unresolved issues from family secrets have a way of popping up in the next generation. Instead of dying with the parents, problems of shame, guilt, anger and unresolved pain are passed on to children and grandchildren. These unhealthy behaviors grow and wreak havoc from one generation to the next. The secrets might be hidden from view, but they don't go away.

Why We Keep Secrets

Just as in the past, the reasons for keeping family secrets today are as varied and unique as the people who keep them. However, when we hide our problems and avoid resolving them, we are prevented from becoming the genuine women God wants us to be. The following scenarios give us some insight as to why people mask their problems by keeping secrets.

Seeking Acceptance

"Being perfect is the only way I can be accepted."

Susan tries to be the perfect mother by pointing out how her children can improve – constantly. She is only being like her own mother, who demanded perfection. Susan has never told her children about the day when she was little and her father left her and her mother. Susan's mother reasoned that her husband would not have left them both if Susan had been a better child.

Fearing Loss

"If I still look pretty, people will adore me."

All her life, Jenny was praised for her beauty. Now in her 50s, she worries about her growing wrinkles and waistline. With her loss of youth and vitality, she is afraid she will also lose the admiration of others, especially her husband. So she compensates by extravagant shopping sprees on the newest cosmetics and trend-setting clothes. She hides her uncontrollable habit and the accompanying bills from her husband.

Escaping Reality

"If I ignore it, the problem will go away."

Clarissa sees her marriage crumbling before her eyes, but she feels helpless to change anything. In public, everything looks fine, but at home, it's a different story. She wishes she could talk to someone, but she thinks no one will listen. Instead, she secretly turns to prescription drugs to dull the pain.

Seeking Emotional Fulfillment

"I'll find love wherever I can."

Gabriella's family spends most of their time at home with a TV, computer or cellphone. They crowd out any conversation or sharing. For company, in the privacy of her bedroom, Gabriella finds solace and excitement in a sexually explicit social media relationship, the closest thing she can get to "love."

Keeping Up Appearances

"If Dad can cheat to get ahead and not get caught, so can I."

For several years, Anne has been misrepresenting her income on her income taxes – until now. This year the IRS is auditing her, and she dreads her fashionable friends finding out about her dishonesty. Anne remembers how her dad took payments "under the table" for his services and never got caught. Now she wonders why her oldest son cheats on tests in school after he found out about his grandfather and mother.

We are at risk for becoming secret-keepers if the right trigger comes along. These triggers include fear, loss, emotional stress or significant life changes. It is important to understand why we are keeping the secrets so we can deal with what is underneath them. We need to ask ourselves some questions. What has happened, and why? Why do I feel the need to keep it a secret? What can be done about it? Would healing and resolution best come within the family? Or would sharing this with a trusted individual outside the family more easily bring me the help and support I need? Should I contact a professional or utilize other resources? Perhaps it is time to start cleaning out our family closets.[1]

Cleaning Out the Closets

Some of us look forward to cleaning out our closets as much as we do to having a root canal. With such a messy, overwhelming task, who knows what we will discover? Sometimes we procrastinate until there is such clutter that we can't close the door. If we can just imagine the end result, we can picture how good our closets will look and how much better we will feel when they are cleaned out. We won't feel that we have to close the door and hide everything. Everything will be freshened up and aired out, organized and in its place (well, at least for a few days!).

The same is true with our family closets. Long-standing secrets sometimes need to be shared. Old heartbreaks need to be mended. Pain needs to be salved. But how do we start?

Face the problem. The mess needs to be tackled. Whatever the reason for the secret, it needs to be addressed and acknowledged. Denial or repression will not work. Understand what the truth is and know it can free you. Although Jesus used this in a different context, the principle is the same: "Then you will know the truth, and the truth will set you free" (John 8:32).

Expose it to the light. Just as you need a strong light in the closet to see what you are doing, so the light of God's Word needs to shine on your problem. "Your word is a lamp to my feet and a light for my path" (Psalm 119:105). Use principles in the Bible to decide what steps should be taken. The goal is not to hang out the dirty laundry for all to see but to discern what would be best to restore relationships with others and, most important, with God. Each situation is unique.

Air it out. Talk to someone. Our overcrowded closets need to be aired out and so do our overburdened souls. If it seems appropriate, open up about the secret to an understanding family member. Approach him or her with "the truth in love" (Ephesians 4:15). If family members are unresponsive to sharing, then tell a close friend or counselor you can trust. Don't live under the heavy burden of secrecy any longer.

Trust God. The outcome might not turn out as you had hoped. Resolution may not come as quickly as you had imagined. Just realize that the first step is only the beginning for healing for you and your family. You cannot change anyone else, but you can change yourself with patience and the Lord's help. Trust Him to work in your life (Proverbs 3:5-6).

Don't put off rattling the skeletons in your closets any longer. You never know what you may find there. In fact, it might get pretty messy! But the sooner you tackle the mess, the sooner you can straighten things out. It can bring the peace of mind that comes with understanding where things are and where they belong. Resolving family secrets will be well worth the effort, and you won't have to hide the skeletons anymore!

Reality Check

1. Why do families keep secrets? When can they become harmful?

2. Why did Abram not want to reveal that Sarai was his wife? Was he entirely wrong in saying she was his sister (Genesis 20:11-13)? How did his secret cause problems?

3. Why do you think Isaac made the same blunder as Abram with his wife, Rebekah? How did Abimelech find out the truth?

4. Why did Rebekah plot with Jacob? What was the result?

5. What secrets did Jacob and Laban keep from each other? What did Rachel keep from both of them (Genesis 31:32-37)?

6. How were Jacob and his sons (including Joseph) involved in keeping secrets?

7. What were the results of David's secret affair with Bathsheba? What was the long-range effect on his family, particularly his sons?

8. What are some modern-day examples of how unresolved family secrets can damage relationships and tear families apart?

9. What are some steps we can take to resolve problems caused by family secrets?

10. Who knows everyone's secrets (Psalm 44:20-21; Hebrews 4:13)?

Secrets in the
Sheep Pen

~

Jacob and his father-in-law, Laban, were not above keeping secrets in the family if it was to their advantage. They both wanted to increase their herds by clandestinely manipulating things to make it happen. Jacob agreed to work for Laban with one stipulation: Laban had to give him every speckled or spotted sheep, every dark-colored lamb, and every spotted or speckled goat. These types were rare, so it did not seem that Jacob was asking for much (Genesis 30:31-34).

Laban left nothing to chance. That day, he gathered all the speckled, spotted and dark types; promptly took them on a three-day journey away from Jacob; and left them with his sons. Such intrigue is something you would expect from Laban.

But Jacob had some secrets of his own. He took the flocks and herds remaining and used a combination of superstition and selective breeding to produce stronger animals for himself.[2] Eventually, Laban owned the weaker animals while Jacob owned the stronger ones. Jacob later acknowledged it was not his own manipulation but rather God who had blessed him and made him prosperous (Genesis 31:9). No matter how many sheep he counted, he could count on God to keep His promise.

Chapter Seven

Making Hospitality
PERSONAL

"Christianity was, and still should be,
the religion of the open door." – William Barclay

D on't you just love getting a letter or card in the mail that is hand-written and addressed to you? My mother called it "friendly mail," and it would be the first thing we would open when the mail arrived. Now our mailboxes more often contain junk mail addressed to that popular but mysterious person with the name "occupant."

These days, mail is not the only thing that is impersonal. Personal service is at a premium with ATMs, self-service checkouts and prerecorded messages. It is an unexpected pleasure to talk to a real person. People pass one another every day and don't even acknowledge that they exist.

In our impersonal world, deep down we all long for something truly personal. As Christian women, we are called, among other things, to offer hospitality in a cold, aloof world that is starving for warm fellowship and personal connection. Greeting one another after worship, in our neighborhoods, or in committee meetings does not provide the time and atmosphere to get to the next level in our relationships.

However, opening our hearts in hospitality is an excellent way to share our lives and get to know one another in a close, relaxed and personal way that other venues do not provide. By seeing where and how others live, we can more clearly understand what is important to them. By taking the time to relate our joys and sorrows, we can better know how to meet one another's needs. By knowing one another better, we can be more transparent with one another. Hospitality provides these opportunities. If we are ever to get real with others and be genuine women of God, we need to open our hearts in hospitality. But just what is hospitality?

Entertaining or Hospitality?

When you think of hospitality, what do you envision? True biblical hospitality involves more than entertaining our friends and setting a pretty table with delicious food. What we might call "secular" entertaining is based on pride. This pride breeds perfectionism and artificiality. Everything has to be just right at the expense of what really matters. Things become more important than people. Making an impression takes precedence over making friends. When we entertain like this, we wear a mask that subtly says: "See how I can impress you with my gourmet cooking, my lovely home, and my clever entertaining. They are an extension of my personality. Everything is perfect. Admire and drool."

On the other hand, biblical hospitality is based on service. It says: "My home and everything I own really belong to God. I will use all of it to serve Him. What I have is yours." Isn't that what the first-century church believed and practiced? Acts 2:44 tells us, "All the believers were together and had everything in common." Their unity, fellowship and love were demonstrated in their idea of hospitality – "What's mine is yours" – so much so that they sold their possessions and gave to those who had need.[1]

Hospitality in the Bible

Hospitality was not a new concept to the first-century church. In fact, it was an ancient custom and obligation for the Egyptians, Greeks and Romans. The Jews considered hospitality a sacred duty. When Abraham hosted three angels who foretold Isaac's birth, he was such an enthusiastic host that he "hurried" and "ran" to begin preparations for his guests' meal (Genesis 18:1-8).

Jesus fleshed out for us the full dimension of hospitality when He told the story of one who showed love to a stranger. Although the top religious leaders of that day – a priest and a Levite – passed by the wounded, half-dead man on the road to Jericho, the Samaritan had compassion on the victim. To the good Samaritan, hospitality involved the sharing of time, effort, medicine, transportation and payment for further care (Luke 10:30-36).

Paul had a firsthand appreciation for hospitality as he traveled from town to town. In Philippi, the Lord opened Lydia's heart to respond to Paul's message by baptism. She offered hospitality to Paul and his company with her invitation, "If you consider me a believer in the Lord ... come and stay at my house" (Acts 16:15). It was important that itinerant preachers and teachers be cared for so they could carry on their work.

Entertaining Strangers?

The logistics of hospitality have changed from the first-century world, but we are still commanded to practice it. In Romans 12:13, Paul admonished: "Share with God's people who are in need. Practice hospitality." How do we practice hospitality today? Are we to fling our doors open to anyone who might venture by, even if we don't know anything about them? After all, doesn't the Hebrews writer tell us, "Do not forget to entertain strangers, for by so doing some people have entertained angels without knowing it" (Hebrews 13:2)?

If we look closely at the context of that verse, we understand that the Hebrews writer was referring to fellow Christians who were traveling and who were unknown to those who could help them. In the first century, inns were expensive and filthy and had bad reputations as hangouts for thieves.[2] In fact, some inns included a prostitute for the night! So they were not good options for traveling Christians who were, for example, displaced because of persecution and needed shelter.[3] The Hebrews writer encouraged brothers and sisters to open their homes to these travelers.

However, our hospitality should not be limited to members of the church (Galatians 6:10). We can use opportunities to show hospitality to people we don't know as well. For example, providing a meal could mean so much to a new neighbor who just moved in, a mother with a new baby, or a family who just lost their home to fire. We also follow in the good Samaritan's footsteps when we pay for someone to eat, sleep or get medical care. For safety's sake, we need to use discretion with those we do not know. John warned against those who might abuse hospitality and directed his readers (including us) to use good judgment and set limits if necessary (2 John 10).

Hospitality at Home

At different times in our lives, we may find ourselves in circumstances not conducive to serving others through hospitality in our homes. Caring for young children or elderly relatives, dealing with a chronic disease, or even struggling to pay the bills on a limited income can all make hospitality more of a challenge. God does not expect more than we can do, but sometimes we just have not made the time or the effort when we could have. We think our hospitality has to be perfect. Instead of offering hospitality, we offer excuses. Let's look at some of these.

"My Home Isn't Good Enough"

Sometimes we think we can't invite people in until we have a beautifully furnished house. If people think they are too good to come to our home, whose problem is it? It is theirs! Make the best of what you have, and enjoy getting to know people. The preacher C.H. Spurgeon said, "It is not how much we have, but how much we enjoy, that makes happiness."

"My Home Is Too Good"

Some people avoid having guests over because they don't want others tracking dirt on their carpet, spilling milk on their floor, or getting muddy fingerprints on their towels. Let's ask ourselves, is this house mine or the Lord's? Does it have to be perfect? We don't have to let people run roughshod over our house, but we can use common sense concerning what God has given us. So put up Aunt Gertie's heirloom figurine and your antique cowbells instead of letting them keep you from opening your home. Remember Jesus' words: "I tell you the truth, whatever you did for one of the least of these brothers of mine, you did for me" (Matthew 25:40). Are we too good to share with Christ?

"I'm a Lousy Housekeeper"

Are you inviting over the White Glove Patrol? Let's get over any guilt complex of thinking we have to be Miss Perfect Susy Homemaker before we can offer hospitality. Have the people you want to invite over never seen dust before? My guess is they have. So it will probably not be a shocking experience if they see it at your house, right?

"I'm a Lousy Cook"

Fortunately, a memorable meal doesn't have to be complicated and time-consuming. A simple one can be just as nourishing and delicious. Perfect one recipe, and make it your standard fare for company. It might take practice if you are like the young bride who proudly presented her first meal to her eager husband. She told him, "Honey, I just know how to fix two dishes – beef stew and lemon pie." After looking at her offering, he replied, "Fine, Dear, which one is this?" [4]

"I'm Shy"

You don't have to be the Lone Ranger. Get others involved by asking your friends and family to help with preparation and cleanup. Share the hostess duties with someone else. You could even invite someone as shy as yourself and make a new friend.

"I'm Too Tired"

Who says you have to serve a seven-course meal from scratch? Try dessert and coffee or tea one evening. Check out grocery store delis and frozen foods. If you haven't had a chance to clean your bedroom yet, close the door. Hospitality is worth the effort. Often you will find yourself revived with a pleasant experience and new friends. Remember what Paul wrote: "Let us not become weary in doing good, for at the proper time we will reap a harvest if we do not give up. Therefore, as we have opportunity, let us do good to all people, especially to those who belong to the family of believers" (Galatians 6:9-10).

"They Didn't Invite Me"

Don't keep a tally of whose turn it is to ask whom over; instead, initiate the invitation yourself. Jesus said: "When you give a luncheon or dinner, do not invite your friends, your brothers or relatives, or your rich neighbors; if you do, they may invite you back and so you will be repaid. But when you give a banquet, invite the poor, the crippled, the lame, the blind, and you will be blessed. Although they cannot repay you, you will be repaid at the resurrection of the righteousness" (Luke 14:12-14). These days people who might not be able to repay us might be college students, a single mother and her children, or a family whose breadwinner is out of a job or in the hospital. There are more folks like these if we start looking.

Hospitality on the Go

Although opening our home is a wonderful way to serve and get to know others, with a little creativity and chutzpah we can also offer hospitality on the go. Jesus is our example of hospitality on the go. He had no earthly home to call His own, yet He provided picnic lunches for thousands. He also served as "chef" at a more intimate seaside breakfast of fish and bread for some of His disciples. Although feeding thousands is probably not in our price range, we can arrange to transport others to a park, river or other scenic location and suddenly even sandwiches taste better.

Try the lovely custom of tea for two (or more). Bring pretty teacups and a real teapot, and brew it as the British do. Serve with crumpets and/or scones, and that lonely widow will have something to remember for a long time. "Lunch Bunches" can also be a lot of fun. Whether you work inside or outside the home, you can take advantage of an hour at lunch to share hospitality with others. Take turns planning where and when to meet, and enjoy the camaraderie. Meet at a restaurant, at the food court in the mall, or in a park. BYOB (bring your own bag) can simplify getting together in a hurry at someone's home or another location. The hostess provides drinks and dessert, and everyone else brings her own sack lunch. Inviting non-Christians you know can enlarge your circle of friends and influence them to seek the Lord.

With our hustling, bustling lifestyles, these mobile ideas can be excellent ways to encourage and get to know one another better. Peter told us, "Offer hospitality to one another without grumbling" (1 Peter 4:9). In effect, he was saying, "No more excuses!" Our table settings do not need to be 100 percent genuine, but our hearts do. However we show hospitality, let's do it with joy. Although it takes some planning, the rewards of fellowship we share in hospitality far outweigh the challenges.

Putting It Into Practice

Although we care for others across the globe, Jesus also called for us to make it personal with someone across the street. We do not want to substitute long-distance caring for the personal attention that hospitality likely implies. When we put hospitality into practice, we might never know the influence we will have on the people whom we touch, but one thing is for sure – our works will live on after we are gone. Paul described the faithful woman in 1 Timothy 5:9-10 as being "well known for her good deeds ... showing hospitality ... helping those in trouble and devoting herself to all kinds of good deeds." Someday may the same good things be said of us!

Reality Check

1. What is the difference between secular entertaining and biblical hospitality? What are some specific ways we can show biblical hospitality today?

2. How did hospitality bring the early church together and help spread its borders (Acts 2:42-47)? Then and now, why is hospitality an important qualification for elders and deacons (1 Timothy 3:2; Titus 1:8)?

3. What were the attitudes of ancient civilizations toward hospitality? What are some ways they showed hospitality (Ruth 2:15-16; Matthew 8:14-15; Acts 16:15)?

4. What specific courtesies did Abraham perform in serving as such a gracious host (Genesis 18:1-10)? How could some of those translate to showing hospitality today?

5. How did the good Samaritan serve as a contrast to the religious leaders of his day (Luke 10:30-36)? How was the Philippian jailer similar to the Samaritan in his hospitality (Acts 16:33-34)?

6. What are some excuses women give for not being hospitable? How can they overcome these excuses to enjoy being hostesses?

7. Why is it important not to worry about being repaid for our hospitality? When will we receive our reward (Luke 14:12-14)?

8. What opportunities do Matthew 25:31-46 provide as examples of how to serve and show hospitality? Whom are we really serving?

9. What are some ideas for hospitality on the go?

10. Can you think of a time when you felt most welcome in someone's home? What did the hostess do to make you feel that way?

"Come on Over!" Hospitality Back When

~

The ancient custom of kindness to strangers probably goes back to nomadic life when people rarely traveled except by necessity. Travelers could only look forward to poor roads, threats from robbers, and few inns. So they typically would wait near the city well or gate for an invitation from someone to offer a place to stay in his or her home. They would expect a host to provide protection, housing and food, often at great effort and expense, because the responsibility of a host was taken seriously (Genesis 19:1-11).

When Abraham's servant was sent to look for Isaac a wife, Rebekah – and later her brother, Laban – provided for him and his entourage. Rebekah ended up becoming Isaac's wife (Genesis 24:26-61). Years later, that same Laban received his nephew, Jacob – Rebekah and Isaac's son – into his home, and Jacob ended up marrying both his daughters and staying 20 years. How's that for a houseguest (Genesis 29–31)? Years later, Reuel welcomed the runaway Moses from Egypt. Perhaps Reuel was eager to find a husband for one of his seven daughters – and he did for Zipporah (Exodus 2:15-22). Do we see a pattern here? Hospitality seemed to be a rewarding way to find a mate!

Chapter Eight

Discovering the
REAL AUDIENCE

"In prayer it is better to have a heart without words,
than words without a heart." – John Bunyon

Several years ago, some clever entrepreneur designed the perfect man who could say just the right thing to make a woman feel special. This creation happened to be a 12-inch doll. With just the touch of his hand, you could hear 16 different phrases, such as "Why don't we go to the mall? Didn't you want some shoes?" or "You know, Honey, why don't you just relax and let me make dinner tonight?" or "The ball game is not important; I'd rather spend time with you."

No wonder this doll is called "Mr. Wonderful"! It's too bad that even though his words initially sound thoughtful, they are coming from a mechanical, non-thinking doll that keeps saying the same things over and over.

The same could be said of some of our prayers! Some people talk to God as if they are talking dolls. They offer the same old phrases to Him without the meaning, humility or gratitude that should accompany their prayers. Instead of being heartfelt and genuine, their requests and thanksgiving come out sounding hollow and rote. How did Jesus feel about prayers like these?

Who Is the Audience, Anyway?

In the Sermon on the Mount, Jesus urged His audience to avoid imitating the hypocrites (the public paraders), who loved to pray in places like the synagogue or street corners, or the pagans (the wordy windbags) with their bombastic prayers. They received their reward when other people saw their grandstanding and verbosity. Rather, Jesus commended the disciple who privately seeks the One who should be our real audience – God in heaven. That disciple will receive his or her reward from a Father who sees in secret (Matthew 6:5-8).

Later, Jesus illustrated this contrast further by telling a story about two men who offered very different prayers, only one of whom pleased God. First, let's look at a modern spin on that story found in Luke 18:9-14:

> Two women come to worship one day.
> They sat right down and began to pray.
> Miss Strut felt so smug and vain,
> So unaware of others' pain.
> She eyed the other woman with scorn
> And then began to toot her own horn.
>
> "Lord, I read my Bible, teach a class.
> I speak to neighbors who I pass.
> I go to lectures, send cheery notes,
> Write missionaries, sew orphans' coats.
> I visit widows, feed stray cats.
> I even keep the preacher's brats!"
> Her windup prayer wound to a close
> As she prided herself with upturned nose.
>
> Across the aisle, Miss Slut's tears flowed
> As she unburdened her heavy load.
> She'd lived a life of sin and shame.
> The courtroom judge knew her first name.
> But she had changed – she was now God's child.
> She was no longer coarse and wild.

She knew how far that she had come;
She thanked the Lord for what He'd done.
"Lord, please forgive me all my sin,
Only through Your grace will I enter in."

Two women left worship from each prayer.
Each had bowed and sought God there.
Just one had nothing left to hide,
Only that one left worship justified.

Can you see the modern-day equivalents of Jesus' parable of the Pharisee and the tax collector? The Pharisee, considered the religious elite of his time, was full of good works but also full of himself. Scripture says he "prayed about himself" (Luke 18:11). On the other hand, the tax collector was thought to be a despicable outcast of society, yet Jesus condemned the Pharisee's prayer and justified the tax collector's. Why? What makes a "good" person's prayer really bad and a "bad" person's prayer good?

We can better understand this if we look closely at the Pharisee's motive. In the Jewish mind, it was more pious to thank God for your righteousness than to take credit for it yourself. The Pharisee was just informing the Lord how good he really was.

Some considered a person to be more righteous if he fasted twice a week. Jewish law dictated only one obligatory day of fasting: the Day of Atonement. But religious Jews like this Pharisee fasted every Monday and Thursday as well. Those days just happened to fall on market days, when crowds from the country swarmed Jerusalem. Those fasting would whiten their faces and dishevel their clothes, demonstrating their piety to everyone they saw.

Mosaic Law prescribed that Jews tithe from all their produce (Leviticus 27:30). This pious Pharisee went above and beyond in that he tithed from everything he had.[1] Although the Pharisee was generous in his gifts, he made a point to let others know about his generosity in his prayer.

The tax collector stood in vivid contrast to the Pharisee. He beat his breast in sorrow for his sins while the Pharisee stood in arrogance. It is possible that the tax collector, seeing himself as unworthy, stood toward the back of the temple while the Pharisee stood up in the more prominent and public front. The tax collector assumed nothing while the Pharisee presumed a great deal. It was the tax collector's attitude of contrition that justified him in God's sight. His prayer was real, heartfelt and humble while the Pharisee's was a wind-up prayer – a long-winded rehearsal of his own self-righteous facade.

How can we, like the tax collector, stand justified in our prayers to the Father? How can we make our prayers real and genuine? How can we cut through any pride and pretense and make our prayers authentic and heartfelt?

Insincerity in Prayer

Let's look first at how we should *not* pray. Several conventions can make our prayers insincere. Here are a few we should try to avoid.

Memorized Prayers

While memorized prayers are not always insincere, they can lose their meaning. This is especially true for mealtime and bedtime prayers. It might be wiser to allow children to say what is on their hearts, even if it takes longer for them to express it. When children pray in their own words, prayers become much more personal. We, as adults, can model this to children by speaking from our hearts and making current, relevant requests and thanksgivings.

Rote Words

Although these are similar to memorized prayers, they are not exactly the same. How often have you heard the same expressions over and over in prayer? We come to expect these overdone expressions with little consideration of their meaning. We may use these worn-out expressions because they are convenient to say, but can you imagine saying the same words over and over to your friends? Yet that is how we sometimes communicate with God. What would happen if we made a point to make our prayers personal and unique each time we said one? We would be less likely to get in a "rote rut."

Archaic Expressions

These expressions are left over from years ago. We might know their meanings, or we might not. We need to put our prayers in our own language so we can understand them. God is not limited to any century of language but delights rather in the language of our hearts, which does not have to be eloquent at all. It is like the little boy who didn't understand the meaning of "to fall short" in a prayer he had heard and then asked, "Lord, forgive us our falling shorts!"

Unkept Commitments

How many times have we said we would pray for someone, and then we did not? It would be better not to commit or to be sure to keep that commitment. It might help to record requests in some way to be sure we do what we say we will do. Some people carry a small notepad to write such requests or use the church bulletin to aid their memory.

Wordiness

Jesus warned that wordiness or vain repetition of phrases is unnecessary: "And when you pray, do not keep on babbling like pagans, for they think they will be heard because of their many words" (Matthew 6:7). Jesus was not being critical of repetition, for He Himself pleaded for His cup to be taken from Him three times in the Garden of Gethsemane (26:39-44). Rather, He was condemning the redundant rhetoric that babbles on and on.

Disbelief

How often do we pray but don't really believe God can fulfill our request? It is much like the early Christians who prayed earnestly for Peter's release from prison. When he miraculously arrived at their doorstep and the servant girl Rhoda told them it was Peter, they thought she was out of her mind (Acts 12:13-16). How would we have reacted if we had been in that crowd? Jesus taught that we must believe before we can receive what we ask for in prayer (Matthew 21:22).

Praying From the Heart

Paul wrote of the sincere prayers of the Macedonians in regard to the Corinthians: "And in their prayers for you their hearts will go out to you, because of the surpassing grace God has given you" (2 Corinthians 9:14). Those heartfelt prayers meant a great deal to the Corinthians and, in a sense, connected them all through prayer. Let's look at some trademarks of a genuine prayer.

Fervency

Remember how Hannah sought the Lord in prayer for a child? "In bitterness of soul Hannah wept much and prayed to the LORD" (1 Samuel 1:10). She poured out her soul in great anguish and grief, and her earnest requests drew the attention of the priest, Eli, and the Lord. She later prayed a prayer of thanksgiving for her son, Samuel.

Frequency

What if our prayers were so frequent that others could count on their regularity? The times of Daniel's prayers were so predictable that the administrators and satraps "caught" him on his knees. His frequent prayers to God condemned him, and King Darius had him thrown into the den of lions. God answered Daniel's prayer for help when an angel shut the mouths of the lions and saved him (Daniel 6).

Focus

Often we are so absorbed with our own needs and worries that our prayers revolve primarily around us. We pray "me and mine" prayers – prayers about my cares, my concerns, my family, my friends. Although these are important, we need to remember others as well. Remember the focus in Jesus' prayer in John 17 as He prayed for His disciples and other believers as well as Himself. We need to think about where we put our focus in prayer.

Faith

In his epistle, James spotlighted the faith of Elijah and told how the prophet prayed earnestly for opposite results at different times – first for a three-and-a-half-year drought and then for rain afterward. The Lord answered his prayer by providing those climatic changes. James wrote, "Elijah was a man just like us" (James 5:17). In other words, Elijah wasn't a spiritual superman but a person who prayed in deep faith. James summarized his point: "The prayer of a righteous man is powerful and effective" (v. 16). Paul reiterated, "Now to him who is able to do immeasurably more than all we ask or imagine, according to his power that is at work within us" (Ephesians 3:20).

We don't have to use fancy words or sacred expressions, because God listens to a humble, obedient heart that wants to do His will. When we cut through the rhetoric, we can sincerely pray with our minds and our spirits. We will want to talk to God as often and fervently as we can. We will confidently believe that He will answer our prayers. When we discover that God is ultimately our real audience, the pretense in our prayers will fall away.

Reality Check

1. Why was the tax collector an unlikely role model in Jesus' parable about prayer? How did the attitude and body language of the Pharisee differ from those of the tax collector?

2. Based on their body language, what kinds of attitudes did the following people display in their prayers: David (2 Samuel 12:15-17); Solomon (1 Kings 8:54); and Jesus (Luke 22:41-44)?

3. What day of fasting was required in the Law of Moses? What two days during the week did some Jews choose to fast, and why?

4. How did the Pharisee in the parable go beyond the required tithing in the Mosaic Law? What was the problem concerning his gift to God?

5. Why might it be better to let children pray in their own words rather than having them recite memorized prayers?

6. Why is it important to make each prayer distinctive and not use rote or archaic expressions when we pray?

7. What are some ways we can be sure to honor our commitments to pray for others when we tell them we will?

8. What was Jesus criticizing when He warned, "Do not keep on babbling like pagans" (Matthew 6:7)? When did Jesus repeat His own prayer (26:39-44)?

9. How should belief play a part in our prayer lives? Why do you think the early Christians were so surprised to see Peter even though they had prayed for such a miracle?

10. What specific steps can we take to incorporate the qualities of fervency, frequency, focus and faith in our prayer lives?

An Unpopular Profession

Jesus' parable about the justified publican's prayer no doubt brought stunned looks to the faces of His listeners because few occupations were more despised. Collecting taxes in any culture has never been popular, but paying tribute to the detestable Romans was an utterly despicable task for the Jews. People classified publicans with other lowlifes of that day. They were coupled with "sinners" (Mark 2:15-16); "prostitutes" (Matthew 21:31-32); and "pagans," meaning Gentiles (18:17). The rabbis believed that one publican in a family tainted the entire family, and they excluded them from serving as witnesses or judges. Exchanging money with them was suspect because their money might have contained stolen currency.[2] While the Jews thought the Pharisees and scribes to be the epitome of righteousness, they thought tax collectors to be the bottom dregs of society and ceremonially unclean.[3]

Yet the Lord was "a friend of tax collectors" (Matthew 11:19). Their eagerness to have a friend like Jesus is evident in how they chose to be with Him in Luke 15:1-2: "Now the tax collectors and 'sinners' were all gathering around to hear him. But the Pharisees and the teachers of the law muttered, 'This man welcomes sinners and eats with them.' " In fact, Jesus chose a tax collector, Matthew, as one of His closest followers (Matthew 9:9-13).

Chapter Nine

Giving From
THE HEART

"If you haven't any charity in your heart,
you have the worst kind of heart trouble." – Bob Hope

In recent years in America, we have seen a media blitz on celebrity philanthropy. Sports pros, entertainers, authors and artists have donated their time and money to their favorite causes. They have used their names to raise an awareness of all kinds of charities. Amazingly, they have raised billions of dollars to help others. People may question their motives by asking if they would give if no one knew about it. Only God knows their hearts, and that judgment belongs to Him.

But we can look at *our* hearts and question *our* motives. Do we give just to look good in front of others? Do we do it only for the recognition we will receive? Would we give if every gift were anonymous – if no one ever knew we were giving? Do we grudgingly donate to causes only so we won't look bad? Or do we give from willing and generous hearts?

Giving to Look Good

Centuries ago, Jesus warned against giving just to look good. In Matthew 6:2-4, He exhorted His listeners not to parade their goodness in front of others:

So when you give to the needy, do not announce it with trumpets, as the hypocrites do in the synagogues and on

the streets, to be honored by men. I tell you the truth, they
have received their reward in full. But when you give to the
needy, do not let your left hand know what your right hand
is doing, so that your giving may be in secret. Then your
Father, who sees what is done in secret, will reward you.

Later, Jesus witnessed just such a scene as He sat teaching in the temple
within sight of the treasury boxes (Mark 12:41). In the temple's Court of
the Women, 13 of these containers were called "The Trumpets" because
of their shape.[1] It is possible that when Jesus spoke of announcing one's
giving with trumpets, He was making a play on words or, more likely,
using a metaphor similar to our expression "tooting his own horn." [2]

As Jesus noted the manner in which the people contributed their
money into the treasury, we can imagine the activity in this busy spot
in the temple. No doubt some of the wealthy, dressed in exquisite robes
and precious jewels, ostentatiously made their way to the Trumpets.
They threw in large amounts of money, making a scene as the jingling
coins landed in the collection box. By caring too much about what
observers thought of them, there was no heart in what they gave.

Small Purse, Big Heart

Perhaps the pompous "coin-jinglers" may have looked down on
the poor widow as she entered the temple. In fact, she may have even
been the recipient of their almsgiving. She pitched in her seemingly
insignificant two mites, the smallest of all coins. Unnoticed by the mill-
ing crowds, she nonetheless was singled out by Jesus because she gave
"everything – all she had to live on" (Mark 12:44). Her gift was excep-
tional no matter how you counted it.

Widows in Palestine were often economically desperate. This poor
widow refused to give into that momentary giver's remorse – "What
will happen if I give and then this happens and ... ?" She had a choice
to give a portion or to give all her money. If she felt obligated, it is
doubtful Jesus would have singled her out because she would have
been no different from the other wealthy contributors.

The important difference between the wealthy and the widow was not
the amount of their gifts. Rather, it was the motivation behind them.
Jesus understood their hearts. Would the Lord have commended the

rich He saw in the temple for giving all they had? No, because they did it just for show. If their hearts had been right, a spirit of generosity would have followed. With their proud and greedy attitudes, it didn't matter how much they gave. Their gifts did not please the Lord.

A Study in Contrasts

What made the widow's gift so commendable while the gifts of the rich fell short? Let's look at some contrasting principles that we can learn from the wealthy and the widow about how to have a giving heart.

Generosity Vs. Greed

Although the rich flaunted their financial independence, the widow demonstrated her total dependence on God by her generosity. She fit Paul's description well: "Each man should give what he has decided in his heart to give, not reluctantly or under compulsion, for God loves a cheerful giver" (2 Corinthians 9:7). What matters is how big your heart is, not the size of your gift.

All Vs. Allotment

The gifts of the rich were only an allotment of their wealth – a contribution hardly to be missed out of so much. The widow's gift was a genuine sacrifice. Although the others paraded their social standing, this widow, who was at the lowest rung of the economic ladder, outgave them by giving all she had. As commentator R. Alan Cole reflects, "It is well to remember that God measures giving, not by what we give, but by what we keep for ourselves." [3]

Faith Vs. Fanfare

It is possible that the widow was ashamed of her gift as small as it was. But it was her faith as well as the proportion of her gift that endeared her to the Lord. Surely she would have been surprised to know how much Jesus thought about what she had given. The rich gave to look good. She looked to God and gave. "For if the willingness is there, the gift is acceptable according to what one has, not according to what he does not have" (2 Corinthians 8:12).

We might not see ourselves as rich in worldly possessions, but we are bountifully blessed compared to so many in the world. Paul's words to Timothy also speak directly to us:

Command those who are rich in this present world not to be arrogant nor to put their hope in wealth, which is so uncertain, but to put their hope in God, who richly provides us with everything for our enjoyment. Command them to do good, to be rich in good deeds, and to be generous and willing to share. In this way they will lay up treasure for themselves as a firm foundation for the coming age, so that they may take hold of the life that is truly life. (1 Timothy 6:17-19)

When we give from our hearts, we can "take hold of the life that is truly life." True living is truly giving.

Ready for a Heart Scan?

If a woman has heart trouble, the doctor will want to run different diagnostic tests to see if her heart is operating at its optimal level. Let the Great Physician run a spiritual heart scan on your heart to see how generous you are in areas that do not involve money. Being willing to give of ourselves – our time, energy and resources – can spill over into how we spend our money. What will your test results be?

- Would you let someone else take the last piece of your favorite dessert?

- Would you let someone else watch a TV show during the time you had planned to watch something?

- Would you let someone with a few items go in front of you in the grocery store checkout line?

- Would you stay late to help a co-worker who needed your assistance?

- Would you let a car get in front of you in traffic if it was safe to do so?

- Would you do "behind the scenes" work that no one sees like cleanup?

• Do you look for opportunities to help your neighbors when they might need it?

• Do you take time to listen to the children and teens in your life?

• Are you patient when you talk with the elderly?

• Do you occasionally volunteer for jobs in church that no one else wants? [1]

We will find that if we are willing to give ourselves, then giving our money will naturally follow. Paul wrote about a group of folks who exemplified this. The Macedonian church overcame great obstacles and considered it a privilege to give beyond their ability and to share with the saints. "Out of the most severe trial, their overflowing joy and their extreme poverty welled up in rich generosity" (2 Corinthians 8:2). How? They gave themselves first to the Lord (v. 5).

Keys to Heartfelt Giving

A giving heart is indeed precious. But how do we develop such a heart? Let's look at some keys that can help us.

Realize that God owns everything. God told Job that "everything under heaven belongs to [Him]" (Job 41:11). We need to understand that we are only stewards of God's bountiful blessings; we are only temporarily taking care of what God has given us. We don't own our possessions – we owe them!

Fall out of love with the world and its stuff. The things of this world just do not last, and they can draw us away from God. "For the love of money is a root of all kinds of evil" (1 Timothy 6:10). "Do not love the world or anything in the world. If anyone loves the world, the love of the Father is not in him" (1 John 2:15).

Learn to be content. Amazingly, wanting less can give us greater joy than having more. Contentment is a priceless gift that cannot be taken from us unless we allow it. "Godliness with contentment is great gain. For we brought nothing into the world, and we can take nothing out of it" (1 Timothy 6:6-7).

Invest in heaven. In today's economy, right when we think we have made both ends meet, someone moves the ends! Although we should monitor our bank accounts, our first priority should be to put stock in things above. Our treasure is in heaven – where thieves, moths and rust can't touch it. Where our treasure is, our heart follows (Matthew 6:19-21).

Be thankful. If we are honest with ourselves, we will see how richly God has blessed us. How compelled we should feel to honor Him by giving whatever we can. We should be "overflowing with thankfulness" for God's goodness (Colossians 2:7). If we really want to feel rich, just think of all we have that money can't buy!

Who Is Really Rich?

Eddie Ogan, a grandmother from Washington, remembers an experience in 1946 when she lived with her two sisters and widowed mother. Their preacher called for a special offering before Easter to be given to a poor family. The four of them decided to buy 50 pounds of potatoes, live on them for a month, and use the $20 they saved to give to the offering.

Soon they thought of other creative ways to save some cash here and there. They saved on the electric bill by turning off the lights and listening to the radio less. One sister cleaned houses and yards for cash. Another baby-sat. Every day they counted their money until they had saved $50 – one $10 bill and two crisp $20 bills – to put in the offering on Easter. They felt so rich as they put their money in the plate.

Later that afternoon, the minister drove up and gave an envelope to their mother. She opened it, and out came $87 with seventeen $1 bills, one $10 bill, and three crisp $20 bills. They were speechless. They were the "poor family"! Before, they had felt like millionaires. Now, they felt poor. They didn't even know they were poor.

The next Sunday, a missionary spoke about an African church that needed a roof for their building made of sun-dried bricks. For only $100, they could buy the materials to enable them to worship even when it rained.

Eddie's family smiled at one another, knowing what they would do with their money. After the offering was counted, the minister announced it was a little more than $100. The missionary was thrilled to receive such a large gift from such a small church and commented, "You must have some really rich people here." Then it struck them – Eddie's family had given $87 of the little more than $100. They were the "rich people" the missionary was talking about! From then on, they never felt poor again.[5]

The truly rich person is the one with the giving heart. May God, the ultimate Giver, give us such hearts!

Reality Check

1. What did Jesus warn against in giving to the needy (Matthew 6:2-4)?

2. How might the phrase "announce it with trumpets" (Matthew 6:2) have been a play on words? How does the expression "tooting his own horn" correlate with this?

3. What did Jesus mean when He said a person should not let her left hand know what her right hand is doing (Matthew 6:3)? How does this teaching impact giving?

4. How did the giving of the rich contrast with that of the widow in Mark 12:41-44?

5. What are some keys to heartfelt giving?

6. In our society, why is it so difficult to be content?

7. Why is it crucial to first give ourselves to the Lord before we can give genuinely from our hearts?

8. How did the leaders of Israel follow David's heartfelt giving to furnish the temple (1 Chronicles 29:2-9)? How can we apply this to our giving today?

9. What is the general principle taught in Proverbs 3:9-10?

10. How can a generous man be blessed by sharing his food with the poor (Proverbs 22:9)? How does Jesus' teaching reinforce this proverb (Acts 20:35)?

Ancient "Social Security" for Widows

Jesus could not have chosen a more surprising example of financial generosity. In those days, a widow often faced an uncertain future. Typically widows were extremely poor and unable to obtain justice (Luke 18:1-5). They were often the object of exploitation and neglect (Mark 12:40). A widow had a better chance at financial security if she had a son who could provide for her. If she had no son, she might still escape poverty by returning to her father's house, marrying again, or remaining unmarried and supporting her family. The book of Ruth provides examples of several of these options.

The Lord made special provisions for widows in the Law. Every third year, widows were to receive a part of the tithes (Deuteronomy 14:28-29). They could also gather gleanings left in the field at harvest (Deuteronomy 24:19-22).[6] Widows wore special garments that distinguished them for these privileges.[7]

The early church provided for widows in different ways, especially for those older than 60 who had no relatives to help them and who had been faithful to their husbands and known for their good deeds (Acts 6:1; 1 Timothy 5:3-10). It is interesting that today the U.S. Social Security system starts at just about the same age.

Chapter Ten

Breaking Up the
HOLY HUDDLE

"What if he meant that we should love our actual neighbors? You know, the people who live right next door." – Jay Pathak and David Runyon

"**T**here she goes again," the elderly lady commented across the fence to her neighbor as they watched their other neighbor speed away in her car. "Taking off with her Bible somewhere."

"Wonder where she's going?" her neighbor mused.

"Probably not to Joe's Bar and Grill," the lady answered, and they both chuckled. "Guess she's headed to church again."

"Do you know where she goes?"

"I don't know, but they must have a lot going on. She's doing something all the time. But if her church is anything like her, I don't want to have anything to do with it. She's too good to have any more than a 'howdy-do' with me!"

Jessica, the neighbor who literally left them in the dust, has a church activity calendar that is full. She is busy with girls nights, seminars, retreats, cookouts, meetings, showers and ladies days. Although she seems devoted to the Lord, Jessica does not seem to have time for her neighbors. She does not seem to care about getting to know them.

Too Busy to Be Neighborly?

It is easy to see how we might be like Jessica, not connecting with those around us. Our lives are over-scheduled and fragmented by our busy lifestyles. When we do socialize, we enjoy spending time with fellow Christians – our "Holy Huddle." Being with other Christians is often like slipping on our favorite pair of house slippers – they make us comfortable, and they fit us great! It's understandable that we would spend more time with people like us.

Often the longer we have been Christians, the more time we spend exclusively with other Christians. That means we spend little or no time with those outside our church fellowship. If we exclude all those who are non-Christians from our circle of friends, we risk harboring a superior attitude about them, much like the "separated" Pharisees had about those outside their fellowship. If we are not open to people outside our fellowship, we might miss the rich friendships we could enjoy and the authenticity we could share – all because we didn't make the effort to get to know them.

Sometimes we are hesitant to take the time to get to know unbelievers because we are afraid they will be a bad influence on us. Paul made this clear in 1 Corinthians 15:33: "Do not be misled: 'Bad company corrupts good character.' " We don't want to be drawn away from God by people who don't love Him.

Yet we are also called to take the good news to the world. How will we ever accomplish that if we do not first show non-Christians we care? That often requires building relationships with them and getting to know them – one friend at a time. Let's look at how Jesus met an unbeliever and how it changed that person's life.

Short on Friends

In Luke 19:1-10, the name Zacchaeus, ironically, means "pure" or "righteous" in Hebrew. That was probably a joke to the people in Jericho, for they thought of Zacchaeus as anything but righteous. He served as the despised chief tax collector of Jericho, probably the local head of other tax collectors. They gathered the taxes and brought them to him. He then passed on what the Romans required, probably skimming off the top for himself and, thereby, making himself a rich man.[1]

Jericho was a good place for Zacchaeus to make his fortune because the city boasted wealth from the great palm forest and famous balsam groves that flourished there.[2]

Many Jews believed that the Roman tax was morally wrong and disloyal to God and that tax collectors were apostates to gather such a tax. The people suspected tax collectors to be extortionists, and often they were. In their position, they could be petty tyrants who few wanted as associates, much less friends.

Zacchaeus might have been "in the money," but he was "out" where people were concerned. He was out of favor with the people because he was considered a traitor who handed over their taxes to the hated Romans. He was out of touch with them as a lonely, social outcast. He was also out of reach as a short man, probably shorter than 5 feet tall,[3] and he just couldn't see over the crowd.

His height had not stood in the way of his rise in business, but it definitely presented a problem in seeing the Messiah as He passed through Jericho one day. With the reputation Zacchaeus had, few would have been willing to let him through, and he might have even been bruised and kicked for his efforts. So this rich man did something very undignified: He climbed a sycamore tree! A relative of the fig tree, the sycamore tree was easy to climb because the limbs were close to the ground.

What compelled Zacchaeus to climb that tree? Did he just want to see a celebrity? Was it because he wanted to be a part of the crowd? Was it that he lived a scrooge-like existence counting his money, and he wanted to see what the hubbub was about? Perhaps he was curious about the Rabbi who talked to and hung out with people like him.

A Big Little Man

To see Jesus was a thrill for Zacchaeus, but to have the Lord stop and call him by name – when He had never met Zacchaeus – proved to the little man that Jesus was special, even a prophet. When the Lord invited Himself to Zacchaeus' home, it showed the tax collector that Jesus wanted to know him better and be his friend. It also showed the people in Jericho that Zacchaeus was worth saving and getting to know.

Jesus broke all the rules with Zacchaeus. To voluntarily associate with a tax collector was considered suspect, and to eat with them, highly questionable. But to invite yourself to someone's house was unheard of! Zacchaeus didn't seem to mind. He felt honored to be able to receive the popular Rabbi in his own home and share his hospitality.

Sharing a meal was an important part of the social life in Bible times. The arrival of any guest like Jesus would have been a festive occasion in what was often the tedium of everyday life. Mealtime was an opportune time for conversation, stories, humor, riddles and music, and during His visit, Jesus might have told parables to entertain and teach His listeners.

Jesus made such an impression that Zacchaeus resolved to give half of his possessions to the poor and pay back four times the amount to anyone he had cheated. His restitution for his extortion went beyond what the Law required (Exodus 22:1-4).

The Jewish leaders believed that tax collectors could never be sons of Abraham. By accepting Zacchaeus, Jesus showed them that God accepted anyone who was willing to change. By taking the time to visit and talk with this little man, Jesus found a big man underneath. That day, Zacchaeus truly lived up to his righteous name.

Breaking out of the Holy Huddle

What if Jesus had not taken the time to stop and notice Zacchaeus? What if Jesus had not gone to his home and visited with him? Jesus focused on Zacchaeus and showed him that he was truly worthwhile. We need to follow Jesus' example and take the time to really get to know people. Who knows but that some will see the love and grace of Jesus through our interest in them and, thereby, want to change their lives and hearts like Zacchaeus?

We need to break out of our Holy Huddle. We need to get to know others who don't know the Savior. Spending time with non-Christians doesn't mean that we neglect our Christian friends but, rather, that we expand our circle of friends. Jesus cherished the 12 apostles as His close friends (John 15:15) and often chose Peter, James and John as His closest companions. Yet He knew that focusing on and getting to know all kinds of people might lead them closer to God. The same is true today. We never know what the Lord can accomplish through these relationships, but first we have to break out of our "Christian cocoons."

Saving Associations

How can we stop ourselves from retreating to the Holy Huddle and develop genuine friendships with those in the world to make our association a saving one?

Be intentional. We need to start by making a conscious effort to get to know others. These relationships are not based on a self-righteous or condescending attitude but on a spirit of friendship. Take time to talk when you see your neighbors outside. Engage the librarian, clerk and committee member in conversation. Plan to try out a new restaurant with a co-worker. Find common ground with non-Christians by participating in the art council, visiting ballgames, quilting, or attending concerts or a children's playgroup. Ask yourself, what can I do today to connect with people around me and bring them to God? [4]

Don't put up invisible fences. Don't limit your friendship possibilities. Sometimes the unlikeliest people can become friends. The people of Jesus' time were shocked when He befriended political rabble-rousers (zealots), dishonest businessmen (tax collectors), and promiscuous women (prostitutes). But Jesus knew how friendships could turn up in unusual places. We need to be open to others of different ages, beliefs, socioeconomic levels and backgrounds and watch how God can work in all our lives.

Be open about your faith. We are not living genuinely if we always hide our faith. It is possible that our friends perceive us as "nice people" without knowing who really controls our lives. If they "accidentally" discover we are Christians, they might wonder why we did not tell them before if the Lord was so important to us. Offer to pray for your friends' needs, and be open about your church involvement. Even those who initially reject you because of your faith could be the very ones later to ask you questions or seek your advice.

Realize not everyone is interested. Not everyone will want to be our friend, but that should not keep us from making an effort. People are busy and often don't want to make time for another friendship. Some are wary of anyone they don't know, or they just don't want to get involved. Other folks feel they have enough friends – they are relationally full. They might be in a different stage of life than us, and we might not have much in common with them. Some just don't want others to get too close for fear of exposure of their personal lives. We have to remember that even Jesus, the perfect Son of God, did not receive a favorable response from everyone He met. Not everyone wanted to be His friend, but this didn't stop Him from opening His heart to all He met.

Focus on a few. Although we want to be friendly with everyone, we may find that we only want to invest in relationships that seem open to our faith.[5] Some people may already be interested in spiritual matters. They may have asked you a question about the Bible or asked you to pray for them. You may find that major changes in people's lives – like a move, a marriage or a new baby – make them more receptive to other changes. Pray every day that God will provide opportunities to open their hearts.[6]

Strike a balance. In spiritual matters, find a balance between interest and interference, sharing and being overbearing. No one wants something crammed down her throat – even if it is good news. A friend will soon feel like a "project" if she is treated that way. We do not want to become a nuisance by preaching and crusading as if we were trying to fulfill some holy quota. If we share the gospel naturally in the course of the day without being pushy and obnoxious, then our friends won't feel like we are religious fanatics who have targeted their next convert.

Be available in tough times. Be there when non-Christians are going through difficult times. Be sensitive to their needs. For example, you might comfort a neighbor who has recently lost her husband. Call the grieving woman. Send her a card. Stop by to visit. Invite her to share a meal or walk with you. If she feels comfortable with it, hug her. If she wants to talk, listen.

Invite non-Christians to church activities. If we truly love people, we will want to bring them to Jesus, just like Philip did. Philip didn't pressure his friend Nathaniel but, instead, invited him to "come and see" (John 1:46). If people know how important God is to us, they will more likely understand why we want to invite them to worship and other church activities. Thom Rainer discovered in his study about peoples' attitudes toward religion that more people than we think are likely to respond favorably to an invitation to church services. If they bring up a past negative experience with your congregation or another church, acknowledge and express regret for the experience. At the same time, look on it as an opportunity to move your discussion to spiritual things if possible.[7]

Make conversion personal. If she really is interested, make opportunities to teach her. Perhaps you have a good book you could share, or you could invite her to a Bible study. Maybe the two of you could meet for a weekly lunch and discuss the Bible. At an appropriate time, think about sharing your own spiritual journey to Christ as Paul did with his listeners in Acts 26:4-18. This makes conversion real. Find the right time and place, and encourage your friend to make a decision about becoming a Christian if she indicates that she is thinking about it.[8]

Avoiding the Holy Huddle will take some time and effort, but it is worth it even if it brings only one soul to Christ. We need to get to know those around us. Who knows – maybe one day a friend will become our Christian sister. As Thom Rainer writes:

> Nearly 60 million people are searching for answers. They are the unchurched next door. They wonder why churchgoers with whom they work and live are silent about their faith. They are waiting on you to open your mouth and your heart.[9]

Reality Check

1. How was the meaning of Zacchaeus' name ironic in light of his reputation as a tax collector? Why did tax collectors have such a reputation?

2. What are several reasons Zacchaeus might have thought he needed a friend? What was unusual about how he and Jesus made the effort to see each other?

3. What are some ways we can be intentional in getting to know people?

4. Although we often feel more comfortable with other Christians, why is it not best to hang out exclusively with them? How can we associate with nonbelievers without being affected negatively by their influence (1 Corinthians 15:33)?

5. How did Jesus socialize with nonbelievers and believers? How is striking a balance crucial in spending time with our non-Christian and Christian friends?

6. Why is it important to be open about our faith early in our relation-ships? How, specifically, can we do this without being overbearing?

7. What are some reasons people might not make the time or effort to get to know us? Why is it wise to be friendly with everyone but to focus on an interested few?

8. What are some specific ways we can be available when non-Christians are going through tough times?

9. Why is it important to invite people to worship and church ac-tivities? What are some ways your congregation can incorporate non-Christians into their activities?

10. How can sharing our personal conversion story be helpful to oth-ers? How does this make our faith real to us and to others?

Publicans, Sinners & Drunks –
Oh, Dear!

~

To a Pharisee, whose name meant "separated," it was especially disconcerting that Jesus associated with anybody and everybody. Perhaps what bothered the fault-finding Pharisees the most was that Jesus not only ate with and welcomed these "great unwashed" but actually seemed to *enjoy* being with them.

As theologian F.F. Bruce puts it:

> He did not associate with them as a condescending benefactor performing a pious duty; he gave the impression that he enjoyed their company – indeed that he chose it by preference, accepting invitations to eat with them and so incurring the reproach of being a "glutton and a wine-bibber, a friend of tax collectors and sinners" (Luke 7:34). … And in parable after parable he drove his lesson home, emphasizing the welcoming grace extended by God to the inadequate and undeserving, the despised and alienated, the insecure and underprivileged. In his teaching and in his example, Jesus' message was one of good news for the outsider.[10]

In the Pharisees' minds, Jesus drew the "worst of sinners" to Him. In Jesus – with His genuine heart of love, compassion and mercy – society's outcasts found a friend.

Chapter Eleven

Saying What
YOU MEAN

*"I am tired of talk that comes to nothing. …
I will speak with a straight tongue." – Chief Joseph*

T hrough the years, men have teased women for not saying what they mean. To prove their point, some unknown author has taken expressions that women say to men and translated them into what women *really* mean. For instance, "Do what you want" really means "You'll pay for this later." Here are a few more "translations":

We need to talk. = I need to complain.

We need … = I want …

You're so manly. = You need a shave, and you sweat a lot.

Do you love me? = I'm going to ask for something expensive.

How much do you love me? = I did something today you're not going to like.

I'll be ready in a minute. = Kick off your shoes, and find a good game on TV.

Nothing's wrong. = Everything's wrong.

For whatever reasons, we sometimes give our words a different spin. However, if we want to be genuine, it's important that we say what we mean and mean what we say. It's like the lady who tried to explain, "I know you believe you understand what you think I said, but I'm not sure you realize that what you heard is not what I meant." [1] Jesus taught about this in the Sermon on the Mount. He warned His listeners to cut to the quick in their conversations: "Simply let your 'Yes' be 'Yes,' and your 'No,' 'No'; anything beyond this comes from the evil one" (Matthew 5:37). That is not always easy to do, especially when you have something difficult to say. Let's look at someone who found the courage to tell it like it was.

Prophet and King

Prophet, adviser, friend – these all described Nathan and his relationship with King David. When David wanted to build the temple, he first told Nathan this deep longing. Nathan encouraged him to do what his heart desired. Through a dream, however, the Lord told Nathan that David's son – not David – would eventually build His temple. Nathan reported the Lord's message to David, but Nathan softened the blow by relaying that the throne of David's son's kingdom would be established forever. Upon hearing Nathan's message, David was undoubtedly disappointed that he was not allowed to honor God in this way, but he also praised the Lord that his son would be so blessed (2 Samuel 7).

Later Nathan had another difficult message to deliver to David. David thought his illicit affair with Bathsheba was covered up and forgotten. Somehow he figured the adultery, deceit and eventual murder of Uriah, Bathsheba's husband, had slipped under God's radar. But God was displeased, and He sent Nathan with a parable for David. David was incensed when he heard Nathan's story of the uncaring rich man who confiscated and killed the pet ewe lamb of the poor man. David ordered that the rich man pay back four times over for the lamb "because he did such a thing and had no pity" (2 Samuel 12:6).

Then you can almost see Nathan pointing his finger at David as he said, "You are the man!" (2 Samuel 12:7). The realization of what he had done must have hit David like a ton of bricks. The prophet added that the sword would never depart from David's house. This was later fulfilled when he lost his first, second and fourth sons – Amnon, Absalom and Adonijah – in a family mire of incest, intrigue and rebellion.

Nathan, however, did not leave without giving a message of hope to David. The king confessed his sin against God, and Nathan told him that God had taken away his sin and that he would not die as he deserved.

When David was old, Nathan showed his loyalty to the king when the prophet learned of Adonijah's concealed attempt to take over the kingdom. Nathan urged Bathsheba to appear before David and remind the king of his promise to Bathsheba. Nathan's action culminated in the failure of Adonijah's ruse and Solomon's elevation to the throne. Nathan played a leading role in the peaceful transfer of power from David to his son Solomon (1 Kings 1). With a true friend like Nathan, it is no surprise that David and Bathsheba named one of their children Nathan (1 Chronicles 3:4-5).

Nathan said what he meant, even if his words could have put him in danger. David could have dismissed Nathan's message, exiled him, and built the temple anyway. The king could have punished or even killed the prophet for exposing his sin with Bathsheba. In Nathan's mission to tell David about Adonijah, he took a chance – what if Adonijah found out and tried to kill him? That didn't stop Nathan. His courage to say what needed to be said – even when it was not the best of news – made him a valued and trusted friend to David. Nathan showed himself to be a confidential adviser, faithful prophet and genuine friend to David. He made the facts plain with no pretense or fabrication.

Nathan serves as an excellent example for us today. Nathan was courageous in speaking when it was not easy and when someone might not like his message. But it was only when he delivered the truth that sin could be dealt with, that damaging secrets could be exposed, and that God's message could be accepted.

Straight Talking

We know we should speak only the truth, but what about times when telling the truth can hurt? How much should we say when we are "speaking the truth in love" (Ephesians 4:15)? Does honesty mean we have a right to speak about everything to everybody? Does telling the truth about a person give us license to malign his or her reputation – in the name of "letting the truth be known"?

How often are we tempted to pretend we are caring when, in reality, we are sharing information that is hurtful and unnecessary? We don't have to tell everything we know or say everything we think. If something goes without saying, let it. We don't need to disclose the intimate details of Aunt Bertha's bunion surgery, even though it really happened. We can choose to say just what is appropriate when it is needed. "A man finds joy in giving an apt reply – and how good is a timely word!" (Proverbs 15:23). "A word aptly spoken is like apples of gold in settings of silver" (25:11).

Even when something is appropriate to share, we need to use discretion. What we say to others might depend on how well we know the person we are speaking with or how indiscriminately she might share with others. Unfortunately, some people cannot be trusted. It's like the three Christian sisters who met together to pray and confess their wrongs to be accountable to one another.

The first one confessed, "I have trouble with flirting with my boss at work."

The second admitted, "I often lie to impress people."

The last one exclaimed, "I can't wait to get out of here because I love to gossip!"

So how do we walk that line between unloading brutal honesty and sidestepping the truth when we say what we mean? How can we say what is appropriate and then zip our lips? Think of the acronym TNT, which reminds us of the explosive power of the tongue (James 3:2-12). This acronym comes from three guidelines Paul outlined in Ephesians 4:

1. Is it **T**rue? Most important, our facts need to be straight (v. 25).

2. Is it **N**ecessary? Do I really have to say it? Will it build people up or tear them down? Some words are just best left unsaid (v. 29).

3. Is it **T**actful? Is it kind? Would I want something like this said about me? (v. 32).

Peeling Back the Layers

If you can trust a person, as Nathan and David trusted each other, it can be a precious relationship. You can learn from each other and help each other. Honesty will rule. Because you care about each other, you can be vulnerable and tell the truth. Sometimes this truth will hurt, but if it is important enough, you can trust this friend to take it and grow from it as David did. A friend kindly chisels down the rough spots of our character as Proverbs 27:17 states: "As iron sharpens iron, so one man sharpens another." Just as Nathan's rebuke of David evoked David's respect for his friend and adviser, so does the wise rebuke: "Like an earring of gold or an ornament of fine gold is a wise man's rebuke to a listening ear" (25:12). "He who rebukes a man will in the end gain more favor than he who has a flattering tongue" (28:23).

It takes time and effort to get close enough to disclose yourself to someone else, but it can be done. Author Harriet Braiker writes,

> It's entirely in your power to regulate the degree to which you peel back the layers of your personality when you disclose yourself to someone. You can keep that person on the surface, or you can allow her to penetrate, by degrees or directly, to the core.[2]

Each of us finds our layer of comfort when we talk to another person. We might disclose more to one person than we would to another. Often we are more likely to say what we mean when we feel comfortable in disclosing who we are. Author John Powell, in his book *Why Am I Afraid to Tell You Who I Am?*, writes about the different conversation levels in which people communicate. We can think about these as comfort levels or layers that we allow others to peel off.

Layer Five: Cliché Conversation

This includes clichés like "How are you? I'm fine"; "I like your dress"; and "Come see us." We say these without expecting any detailed replies. We exchange them to be courteous, but we usually do not get involved in any deep, penetrating communication. If we did, we would be surprised!

Layer Four: Factual Reporting

This is just repeating what we know about others with no personal commentary of our own. At times this is innocently informative; at other times this can degenerate into downright gossip. We neither share much of ourselves nor invite much of others.

Layer Three: Personal Ideas and Judgments

This is only the beginning of sharing, but it is a start, even if it is only our judgments and decisions. Our communication is strictly censored. We watch one another closely. What do we think of one another? We want to be sure we will accept one another, or we will quickly retreat.

Layer Two: Personal Feelings

When we share our feelings or emotions, we are telling why we feel the way we do. This distinguishes us from other people, for no one will feel exactly as we do about everything. If we can share on this "gut level," others will have a lot better idea of who we are and what we mean.

Layer One: Peak Communication

This layer is closest to our hearts. On this deepest level, there is absolute honesty and openness. We share mutual empathy. This says that we accept one another – warts and all.[3]

Open and Honest

Clearer communication – being open and honest – can make us healthier. As Powell writes:

> We either speak out (report) our feelings or we will act them out. ... We do not bury our emotions dead; they remain alive in our subconscious minds and intestines, to hurt and trouble us. It is not only much more conducive to an authentic

relationship to report our true feelings, but it is equally essential to our integrity and health.[4]

This "mind/body connection" plays a part in the way our body reacts to our feelings. If we always hide how we feel, we may develop physical problems like ulcers, headaches, insomnia, high blood pressure and weight gain – just to name a few.[5]

Not every communication between people will be peak communication, nor would we want it to be. Being honest and vulnerable isn't easy. We will not feel close to everyone. Yet the more open we are, the better chance we have to be closer in our relationships to people. As author Clinton McLemore writes, "Without sharing what is going on inside of us, there can be no true fellowship." [6] This sharing will be worth the trouble when you find another person who can really care about you and share your joys and burdens.

This is the challenge we as Christian women face. Brenda Waggoner writes:

> To be Real, to be authentic, is not always pleasant. It doesn't make sparkling light dinner conversation, and you cannot unmask all your pain with every acquaintance. But those of us who are unwilling to settle for superficial spirituality must learn to be honest with ourselves and with God. And we all need someone with skin on ... with whom we can open up and be vulnerable.[7]

May we be the kind of women "with skin on" who can be honest as we speak and empathetic as we listen to whatever difficult things others may share. As Ruth Bell Graham once urged, "Just pray for a tough hide and a tender heart." [8] That is wise advice for saying what we mean.

Reality Check

1. What role did Nathan play in King David's court? What difficult message from God did Nathan deliver to David when the king wanted to build the temple, and why?

2. How did Nathan convict David of his sin with Bathsheba? Why do you think Nathan's parable about a lamb evoked such an emphatic reaction in David?

3. Although David's sin was punishable by death, why was his life spared? How was David punished instead?

4. Later, how did Nathan show his loyalty to David? What was the result of Nathan's warning?

5. How was Nathan exemplified in Proverbs 17:17; 25:12; and 28:23?

6. What are three practical guidelines to help us speak the truth in love to others (Ephesians 4:25, 29, 32)?

7. How far should a woman go to be truthful? How can brutal honesty become a pretense in itself?

8. How can clearer communication with others help us be healthier? What happens when we try to bury our emotions?

9. What are the five conversation levels in which we communicate? What is the value in each level?

10. Why is it sometimes difficult to peel back the layers of our lives to others and be vulnerable? How can we make it easier for others to open up in this way?

Foretelling & Forthtelling

The prophet Nathan belonged to a distinguished, if not always popular, profession. Just say the word "prophet," and who comes to your mind? Elijah? Daniel? John the Baptist? How about Noadiah or Anna or the four daughters of Philip? Several prophetesses appeared at pivotal times in the history of God's people. Miriam led the women in praising God for saving them from the Egyptians and the Red Sea (Exodus 15:20). Deborah accompanied Barak, who led a victorious army over the Canaanite king Jabin (Judges 4). Huldah prophesied of Judah's upcoming destruction and prompted Josiah's renewal of the covenant (2 Kings 22:14-20).

The work of prophets and prophetesses could be summarized in two labels: foretelling and forthtelling. We often remember prophets for foretelling; that is, predicting events that were to come. If their prophecies did not come true, then they were considered false prophets (Deuteronomy 18:21-22). But prophets were also designated to tell forth the words of God and decry the injustices and sin of the society in which they lived. They spoke out against hypocrisy of their day and demanded the return of justice, mercy and righteousness. Although each messenger was as unique as his or her purpose, they all served a valuable role in foretelling and forthtelling God's message to His people.

Chapter Twelve

Bursting
INFLATED PRIDE

"Nothing is as hard to do gracefully as getting down
off your high horse." – Franklin P. Jones

One year on Mother's Day, my daughter, Amy, gave me a helium-filled foil balloon. Usually balloons like that lose their air after a few days, but somehow this one has stayed inflated for more than a decade! Somehow the pressure inside has remained constant within the balloon.

In a spiritual sense, our pride can be just like that balloon. We can have a healthy pride in who we are and what we accomplish. When someone or something puts us down, that pride can be deflated, and we can lose our confidence. On the other hand, if we get too "high" on ourselves and our confidence gets blown out of proportion, our pride can be inflated to a reckless level. When it reaches that state, the balloon bursts! In either situation, pride can give us an artificial view of ourselves and others. To reach spiritual equilibrium, we need to keep a healthy balance between deflated confidence and overinflated pride.

Unfortunately, the human race has been known to get pretty vain and arrogant. As politician Alan K. Simpson quipped, "Those who travel the high road of humility are not troubled by heavy traffic." [1] It is especially easy for those in positions of authority to feel bigheaded. Let's focus on a king who was puffed up and proud. The Lord found a reason to burst his self-important bubble.

Pride Before a Fall

Nebuchadnezzar was a king with a dream – literally. In fact, this king of Babylon seemed to have a lot of dreams. To his royal frustration, his magicians, enchanters, astrologers and diviners could not explain them, but the Jewish exile Daniel could interpret dreams through the help of the Lord. Nebuchadnezzar was especially baffled about a tree that was once fruitful but then was cut down and stripped of its fruit with only its stump and roots remaining. The king called in Daniel to interpret his dream (Daniel 4:1-18).

At first Daniel was terrified at the dream's meaning and did not want to answer the king. With the king's urging, Daniel answered that the tree represented Nebuchadnezzar in all his strength and greatness. But later the king would be driven away from people to live with the wild animals. He would eat grass with his body drenched with dew, his hair growing like an eagle's feathers, and his nails growing like a bird's claws. To top it all off, this would last for seven years. Daniel urged Nebuchadnezzar to "renounce [his] sins by doing what is right, and [his] wickedness by being kind to the oppressed. It may be then that [his] prosperity will continue" (Daniel 4:27).

Nebuchadnezzar had a year to follow Daniel's advice, but he did not heed it. Instead, he continued in his pomp and pride. He was a prolific builder with magnificent projects in Babylon, including temples and streets. He channeled the Euphrates River through the city in a series of canals. He built a luxurious palace furnished with the finest materials and a terraced palace garden, which gained international acclaim as one of the seven wonders of the ancient world.[2]

One day as Nebuchadnezzar walked on the roof of his palace, this prideaholic said to himself, "Is not this the great Babylon I have built as the royal residence, by my mighty power and for the glory of my majesty?" (Daniel 4:30). While the words were still on his lips, God told him that he would receive the judgment prophesied in his dream. Immediately, Nebuchadnezzar was driven away just as Daniel had foretold.

At the end of that terrible time, Nebuchadnezzar raised his eyes in praise and honor to God. He acknowledged that while all men are as nothing, God is all-powerful and "no one can hold back his hand" (Daniel 4:35). This declaration was amazing coming from a pagan king, but he had been disciplined from the Lord's hand, and he had received grace by that same hand. God allowed Nebuchadnezzar to renew his leadership and reign in even greater power than before. The Jews in Babylonian captivity at this time could only be amazed by their God, who could humble even the greatest ruler. For the king himself proclaimed, "Those who walk in pride he is able to humble" (v. 37).

Nebuchadnezzar was successful in many ways, but the Lord humbled him when he did not give God the glory for his success. Nebuchadnezzar exemplified this proverb: "Pride goes before destruction, a haughty spirit before a fall" (Proverbs 16:18).

What About Us?

Hopefully, we will not have to grow feathers and eagle's claws like Nebuchadnezzar to learn not to be proud. But how often do we achieve some good thing and not give the Lord the credit? We can have a healthy appreciation and pride in what we accomplish. The problem comes when our pride prevents us from acknowledging God's help in whatever we do. It is through the Lord that "we live and move and have our being" (Acts 17:28). We can do nothing without Him. It is easy to think too highly of ourselves, especially when we succeed at some goal or attain some possession. There are so many areas in which our pride can take over. Let's look at some of them.

Intellect

Some women are puffed up because of their high I.Q. They are the first to tell you their high score on a college test or quick comprehension of the answer to a difficult puzzle. Other women are proud of their low intelligence. They revel in their ignorance and don't want anyone to expect anything more from them.

Appearance

Many women glory in their beauty as they strut and preen themselves like peacocks. They lose a big sense of their identity when they start to age and their appearance changes.

Talents

It is a real temptation for women to boast about their talents, whether demonstrated in their jobs, their hobbies or their volunteer work. For some, this is the only recognition they receive in their lives, and they are hungry for it.

Money

A woman's bank account can give her a false sense of pride. Some women brag about how much money they make while other women take a superior attitude about their money-saving savvy in bargain hunting.

Possessions

What a woman owns often owns her. How many women pride themselves in their furniture, cars and clothes as they let others know where they bought them and how much they paid.

Age

Ladies can wear their age like a badge of honor. Young ones show off their figures, boyfriends and dress sizes while older ones brag about their retirement homes, exotic vacations and leisure time.

Family

Family pride can be a priceless yet prickly thing. Children are a gift from the Lord, and they can give us so much joy. Yet family pride can mushroom out of proportion as some women go on and on about the child's latest grade, prize or accomplishment.

Faith

Some Christians take too much pride in their faith. They feel smug in comparison to others in their religious family heritage, their good works, and the number of years they have been members of the church.

Humility

Some are even proud of their humility! They pride themselves in looking and acting humble. They think that their humility is better than someone else's pride, and that, by the way, is their humble opinion!

Some anonymous wit has observed, "When God made man he didn't arrange the joints of his bones so he could pat himself on the back." [3] Clearly God is not pleased with our pride: "The LORD detests all the proud of heart. Be sure of this: They will not go unpunished" (Proverbs 16:5).

A Lesson in "Self"

If we look again closely at Nebuchadnezzar's statement, we will see the key to his pride: "*I* have built ... by *my* mighty power ... for the glory of *my* majesty" (Daniel 4:30, emphasis added). This presumptuous king had a "me, my, mine" problem in which his focus was only on himself. We can have the same problem if we dwell only on ourselves and what we have done. If we check out the dictionary entries that begin with the word "self," we will see how far some of these extremes can take us on the scale of pride:

- "Self-centered" – The world revolves around me.

- "Self-promoting" – Look what I have done!

- "Self-righteous" – I'm so good (and you're not so great)!

- "Self-satisfied" – I don't need anyone's help, because I've got it covered.

In a world that fosters the importance of self-identity and the self-made individual, we can see how easy it is to fall into the "me, my, mine" trap. But the same word in the dictionary provides a remedy to the problem as well.

- "Self-assurance" – I don't have to feel inferior, because God makes me special.

- "Self-denial" – You come before me – go ahead.

- "Self-respect" – I'm okay because God loves me.

If we have a healthy sense of self-worth, we have achieved that spiritual equilibrium between too much and too little pride.

Finding Spiritual Equilibrium

If we are ever to find a balance between inflated and deflated pride, we need to continually examine our hearts. Nebuchadnezzar was pretty blatant in his pride, but sometimes we may find pride slipping into our hearts in more subtle ways. Do we ever put ourselves down so others will praise us? Although we may not tell them directly, do we make certain that others see evidence of our accomplishments so they will praise us? Do we refuse to admit fault or listen to advice because "we are fine just the way we are"? Pride can pop up in unusual ways, but people can see through it and so can God. As American author Thomas Merton observed: "Pride makes us artificial; humility makes us real." So how can we get rid of pride?

Boast only in the Lord. In a beautiful passage, the prophet Jeremiah explained that our boasting should not come from our wisdom, strength or riches but rather from our understanding and knowledge of the Lord (Jeremiah 9:23-24). Centuries later, Paul proclaimed that Jesus is our all in all as he paralleled Jeremiah's thought: "Therefore, as it is written: 'Let him who boasts boast in the Lord' " (1 Corinthians 1:31). We don't need to boast in anyone or anything else.

Put the future in God's hands. The writer James exhorted his listeners to plan within the Lord's will and not brag about the future (James 4:13-17). Because we can't count on anything tomorrow except the Lord, any bragging about what we will do amounts to only empty words. "Do not boast about tomorrow, for you do not know what a day may bring forth" (Proverbs 27:1).

Let others praise you. When we do well, we need not flatter ourselves or blow up our own egos. If others want to praise us, we can accept their congratulations graciously without becoming pompous braggarts. God is not the only one who hates pride – other people don't care for it either. Folks who sing their own praises usually perform with no accompaniment. "Let another praise you, and not your own mouth; someone else, and not your own lips" (Proverbs 27:2). As Gene Brown has wisely noted, "The really tough thing about true humility is you can't brag about it!" [4]

Develop your God-given talents. The Lord has given each of us talents to serve Him and others. If we develop these gifts, we can have a healthy pride in ourselves. We won't have to constantly compare ourselves to others, because each of us can make our individual, God-blessed contribution to the world (Romans 12:3-8).

Be thankful to God. We have so much to be thankful for, and we receive it all from the Lord. "Every good and perfect gift is from above, coming down from the Father of the heavenly lights, who does not change like shifting shadows" (James 1:17). How can we boast when He deserves all the glory?

Humble pie is sometimes hard to swallow, but swallowing our pride seldom gives us indigestion. We can learn humility from the best example of all: Christ. Paul charged us to "do nothing out of selfish ambition or vain conceit, but in humility consider others better than yourselves. Each of you should look not only to your own interests, but also to the interests of others" (Philippians 2:3-4). The apostle then asserted that our attitude should be the same as that of Christ, who humbled Himself (vv. 5-11). Only through our Lord can we overcome our overinflated pride and find our spiritual equilibrium.

Reality Check

1. How can deflated pride be as much of a problem as overinflated pride? Who is at the center of each of these problems?

2. Who was Nebuchadnezzar? What were the accomplishments that led to his pride?

3. Why was Daniel afraid to relay his interpretation of Nebuchadnezzar's dream to him? What eventually happened to the king?

4. What other kings let pride precipitate their downfall (2 Chronicles 26:16-23; 2 Chronicles 32:24-31)?

5. In what areas can pride affect women's lives today?

6. Why is it important to develop our God-given talents?

7. Why is it sometimes difficult to receive a compliment with the right attitude?

8. What are some things we can boast about in the Lord (Psalm 44:8)?

9. Who is our ultimate example of humility? What qualities make Him worthy of our imitation (Philippians 2:5-11)?

10. Why was Paul's admonition to boast in the cross of Jesus Christ in Galatians 6:14 so incredulous to the people at that time? What was the cross a symbol of in that culture?

Kingly Power
& *Pride*

Nebuchadnezzar was not the only king throughout history whose power drove him to pride. After all, when a monarch has absolute authority, it often goes to his head. For example, when the people shouted that King Herod was a god, he grew puffed up and did not give praise to God. An angel of the Lord struck him down, and he was eaten with worms and died (Acts 12:21-23).

In contrast to pagan kings, Israelite kings were limited in their power. God held them responsible to the people they served. Newly crowned kings Saul and David made agreements with the people (1 Samuel 10:25; 2 Samuel 5:3). Unlike kings who disregarded the poor, the kings of Israel were to support the rights of the poor and judge in their favor.

Ultimately, the Lord was Israel's true King. The kings God chose were called to account when they trespassed His Law. When David desired Bathsheba and committed adultery and murder to have her, he tried to cover up his sin. God sent Nathan the prophet to make David accountable. On the other hand, when the Persian king Xerxes' pride was hurt by Vashti and he wanted another queen, he just rounded up the beautiful young virgins of the land and took whomever he wanted (Esther 1–2).

Chapter Thirteen

Finding Your
ULTIMATE
Security

"A hallmark of security in Christ is confidence." – Julianna Slattery

S usan was the woman everyone called on to get things done. She was the first one considered in the school parent association if a fund-raising project needed to be organized. Susan was also at the top of the list of volunteers for accomplishing things in her congregation, whether it was organizing vacation Bible school, a ladies retreat, or the church library. Her husband often complained that she was overcommitted, but she sincerely felt her service was a way to use her talents.

Then without warning, Susan's mother died, and she was responsible for settling the estate. She had to give up her volunteering for several months. During that time, she was able to slow down and think about her past and future. Although she felt blessed in many ways, insecurities of feeling left out and unaccepted from her childhood still gnawed at her. Now that her days were not filled with demands on her time and energy, she began to doubt her worth. She felt useless and wondered if people would still appreciate her if she wasn't completing some task for them.

She took a hard look at why she volunteered so much. Was it to fill a need in the school or church? Or was it to fill _her_ need to be in charge, find affirmation and feel good about herself? She discovered that her identity and confidence were bound up in her volunteering. She found that even in doing good things she was putting on a show. She was basing her confidence in what she had done instead of what God had done for her.

Paul's World-Based Confidence

Much like Susan, Paul had a confidence that was centered on what he did. No one could doubt that he was exemplary in his religion. He grew up with every advantage and learned at the feet of the best of teachers. He earned the respect of the leaders of his day. He had impeccable morals and was extremely zealous in his beliefs.

However, an encounter with Jesus literally blinded Paul and eventually enlightened him. He discovered that he was actually fighting against God – the One he sought to serve. The original basis of his worth was shattered. He discovered that his confidence in his education, pedigree, religious heritage and accomplishments was misplaced. From the world's perspective, these were important in a successful rabbi's career, and Paul had taken on the world's thinking. When he learned the truth of his error, he abandoned his world-based confidence and put his confidence in the Lord:

> If anyone else thinks he has reasons to put confidence in the flesh, I have more: circumcised on the eighth day, of the people of Israel, of the tribe of Benjamin, a Hebrew of Hebrews; in regard to the law, a Pharisee; as for zeal, persecuting the church; as for legalistic righteousness, faultless. But whatever was to my profit I now consider loss for the sake of Christ. What is more, I consider everything a loss compared to the surpassing greatness of knowing Christ Jesus my Lord, for whose sake I have lost all things. I consider them rubbish, that I may gain Christ and be found in him, not having a righteousness of my own that comes from the law, but that which is through faith in Christ – the righteousness that comes from God and is by faith. (Philippians 3:4-9)

Once Paul experienced real identity and worth in Jesus, he wanted to leave the former things behind. He was even willing to throw all his assets on the garbage heap. He discovered that his liabilities were really his strengths. By relying on God's power and admitting his own weakness, he could say, "For when I am weak, then I am strong" (2 Corinthians 12:10).

Why We Join the Masquerade

Like Paul, we can still rely on our own resources to make it in life. We depend on our assets to set us apart from the crowd. We find our value as Christians in "worthy things" like our talent, background, spiritual life and good record. We trust that our strengths will carry us through.

The world reinforces this fallacy. Some psychologists tell us to repeat self-affirmations to psyche ourselves up, such as "I'm strong enough to handle whatever comes my way"; "The answers to all my needs lie within me"; and "I'm a powerful person." One problem rests with these statements: They are just not true! In fact, they can have the opposite effect on our confidence. When a crisis bombards us, we discover we cannot handle everything by ourselves. Our world-based confidence falls flat. We grow even more insecure.

Many of our insecurities are born in childhood and rear their ugly heads in adolescence. In adulthood, they often hover below the surface unless they have been dealt with in a healthy way. Many of us struggle with self-esteem issues and do not entirely know why. We let the "tapes" in our minds determine our personal value. These replays of our life experiences undermine our confidence.[1]

Insecurity is a principal reason we hide behind masks. Ultimately, we don't feel confident. We feel like we won't measure up. We are afraid we will look inadequate in front of someone else. Because we can't be good at everything, there will probably be times when we will look inadequate. So we join the masquerade to hide our insecurities instead of facing and dealing with them. We build a layer of world-based confidence to shield us and try to "fake it till we make it." When we hide behind masks, we find our worth is determined by a temporary worldly reality, and the charade is complete.

Who Determines Our Worth?

The world extends this masquerade by basing our self-worth on several erroneous concepts. In our dog-eat-dog world, life is a competition with losers and winners. By the world's standards, some people are more valuable than others. An unborn child is discarded while a beautiful, talented actress is worshiped. The world tells us that our worth is something we achieve by virtue of an advantageous birth, profitable portfolio or prestigious title in the company. In this world-view, other people can determine our worth, and they can change their opinion in a heartbeat. If we don't "perform" well, if we lose our job, if we grow older – all these can cause others to treat us differently.

On the other hand, as Christians we know that the basis for our worth and confidence comes from the Lord. According to the Bible, we can't *achieve* self-worth. Why? Because we already have it! God loves and values us no matter what we achieve (1 John 4:9-11). It doesn't matter what we look like or where we came from. Nothing can take away our worth because God made us in His image (Genesis 1:26-27). We each were created with an eternal soul that will never die.[2]

God loves us so much that He actively seeks a relationship with every one of us. With God, we don't have to put on a show. When we seek an open, trusting relationship with God, we begin to appreciate our true value. A.W. Tozer describes this "see all, know all" relationship well:

> Some of us are religiously jumpy and self-conscious because we know that God sees our every thought and is acquainted with our ways. We need not be. God is the sum of all patience and the essence of kindly good will. We please Him most, not by frantically trying to make ourselves good, but by throwing ourselves into His arms with all our imperfection, and believing that He understands everything and loves us still.[3]

When people do not invest in that fulfilling relationship, they often try unsuccessfully to fill a God-shaped void with themselves. In our narcissistic world, this "all about me" attitude is often paraded in TV and movie personalities. We see "beautiful people" giving interviews, endorsing products and gracing magazine covers. They seem to hold the world in their hands, and in turn, the world considers them valuable. Fast forward a few years, and we may wonder what happened to them.

When we let other people determine our worth, our value supposedly seesaws up and down with our looks or popularity. But we know that God determines our value. When Jesus died on the cross for us, He purchased us with His own blood, and that makes all of us very special and worth a great deal. Through His sacrifice, we are loved, redeemed, precious, chosen, treasured and forgiven! We can feel God-confident because of our relationship with Him and His purpose in our lives.

Although the world gives us a skewed image of ourselves that depends on outer criteria, God makes us valuable through His Son, Jesus Christ. Through Jesus, we see how truly unworthy we were as sinners separated from a righteous and holy God (Romans 3:10-12). Yet we are made righteous through faith in His Son (Philippians 3:9). As we grow in the Lord, we realize that it isn't that we are good but that God has been so good to us. Instead of experiencing insecurity because of our guilt and inadequacies, we find our worth and confidence in the Lord. Then we can better understand who we are and who God made us to be.[4]

Beyond the Masquerade

So how can we tap the courage to put our confidence in God? How can we leave the masquerade behind and live genuinely in Christ? In Colossians 3:1-4, Paul answered these questions when he wrote about where the focus of our authenticity should be:

> Since, then, you have been raised with Christ, set your hearts on things above, where Christ is seated at the right hand of God. Set your minds on things above, not on earthly things. For you died, and your life is now hidden with Christ in God. When Christ, who is your life, appears, then you also will appear with him in glory.

If we are to be genuine women of God, we need to act and think less like the world. When you think about it, any mask we might wear is a facade designed to make us look different in the eyes of the world. Whether it is to please others or to look better than we are, we are trying to meet the world's standards. When we don masks of pride, deceit or snobbery, we may fool the world but not God. These masks separate us from the One who made us and loves us.

However, as we learn to live beyond the masquerade and become more like the Lord, earthly things start to lose their glitz and glitter. We don't feel such a need to impress others, because we know the things of the world won't last. Our whole outlook is different. Our hearts and minds focus more on eternal things, not temporary earthly things. Although our feet are on the ground, our hearts are in heaven.

So instead of hiding behind masks, we can be hidden by something much better: Jesus Christ. We do not have to try to be something we are not, because we know *whose* we are. Christ is our life! We can feel safe and secure in our true identity. We can know the comfort, like David, of being hidden and protected by the shadow of His wings (Psalm 17:8). Although we are imperfect, we can feel confident in Christ even as we approach our Almighty Father (Hebrews 4:16). "Let us draw near to God with a sincere heart in full assurance of faith" (10:22).

Jesus the Authentic

What an awesome Savior we have! As our ultimate example of authenticity, He experienced the limitations of being human. He was a man who felt what humans feel. He was tired, hungry, lonely and rejected. He felt pain, and He suffered. Cruel, sinful people crucified Him. Yet He was also divine. He rose from the dead and ascended back to heaven. He promises to take us there to be with Him if we live a genuine life like His. In His divinity, He triumphed over death. This reality – the risen Savior – is the essence of our life. We will share in that glorious resurrection someday! As Paul wrote in Colossians 2:17, "Reality … is found in Christ." When we want to get real, it doesn't get any better than that!

Reality Check

1. Although Paul was sincere, where did he base his confidence? What experience helped to change his heart?

2. Why is it easy for us as Christians to place confidence in the good works we do for God?

3. Why is it dangerous to rely on the world-based self-affirmations mentioned in the chapter? How can God-based affirmations from the Bible (for example, Psalm 56:11; Romans 8:37 and Philippians 4:13) be used to genuinely bolster our confidence?

4. Why do you think many of our insecurities are born in childhood and surface in adolescence? Why do some remain unresolved into adulthood?

5. Why is insecurity a principal reason we join the masquerade?

6. What are some erroneous concepts on which the world bases people's worth? What are some current examples of how the world values people?

7. What does the fact that God made us in His own image tell us about our value (Genesis 1:26-27)?

8. What demonstrates how much God values us (John 3:16-17; Ephesians 3:16-21; 1 John 3:1)?

9. How does being hidden in Christ change how we think about worldly things?

10. How do the authenticity of Christ's life and the reality of His resurrection give us hope now and for eternity?

Confidence
in a
Cause

~

The apostle Paul was so confident (read: fanatic) in his Jewish religion that he killed those who did not agree with him. It took an encounter with the risen Savior to turn his world upside down and change his heart. In a short time, the "hunter" became the "hunted." He who once killed Christians was now willing to die for that cause.

The roots of Paul's religious zeal started early. Like other Jewish boys, he probably studied the Torah at the age of 5, the Mishnah at 10, and the Talmud at 15. He studied at the feet of Gamaliel, the famous Jerusalem rabbi. Paul grew up a Pharisee, the son of a Pharisee, which implied his father or ancestors were Pharisees.

This "Hebrew of Hebrews" was headed for a bright future in the Jewish faith (Philippians 3:5). Paul put his confidence in his preparation, but it took Christ to show him where it truly belonged. Paul later penned: "Such confidence as this is ours through Christ before God. Not that we are competent in ourselves to claim anything for ourselves, but our competence comes from God" (2 Corinthians 3:4-5). May we also find that confidence in God and an authenticity that lies beyond the masquerade.

Endnotes

Chapter 1 – Canceling the Show of Pretense

1 Michael Ventre, "Just How Real Are Reality TV Shows?" NBCNEWS. com, 14 Apr. 2009 <http://today.msnbc.msn.com/id/30092600/ns/today-entertainment/t/just-how-real-are-reality-tv-shows/#.TwnxexzZh0g>.

2 William Barclay, *The Gospel of Matthew, Volume 2* (Philadelphia: Westminster Press, 1975) 288.

3 F.F. Bruce, *Paul: Apostle of the Heart Set Free* (Grand Rapids: Eerdmans, 1977) 49.

4 Barclay 283-84.

5 Spiros Zodhiates, ed., The Complete Word Study Dictionary: New Testament (Chattanooga: AMG, 1992) 197.

6 Robert H. Mounce, *New International Biblical Commentary: Matthew* (Peabody: Hendrickson, 1991) 215.

Chapter 2 – Spotting a Fraud

1 Everett Ferguson, *Backgrounds of Early Christianity* (Grand Rapids: Eerdmans, 1987) 407-08.

2 John Fischer, *12 Steps for the Recovering Pharisee (Like Me)* (Minneapolis: Bethany, 2000) 46.

3 Craig S. Keener, *The IVP Bible Background Commentary: New Testament* (Downers Grove: InterVarsity Press, 1993) 109-10.

4 Richard France, *The Gospel According to Matthew (New International Commentary on the New Testament)* (Grand Rapids: Eerdmans, 1985) 325.

5 Phil Callaway, *Who Put the Skunk in the Trunk? Learning to Laugh When Life Stinks* (Sisters: Multnomah, 1999) 147.

6 Brennan Manning, *Posers, Fakers, and Wannabes: Unmasking the Real You* (Colorado Springs: NavPress, 2003) 97.

Chapter 3 – Dodging the Snob Mob

1 Croft M. Pentz, *The Complete Book of Zingers* (Wheaton: Tyndale, 1990) 249.

2 Clyde Murdock, *A Treasury of Humor* (Grand Rapids: Zondervan, 1967) 9.

3 Marion Leach Jacobsen, *Crowded Pews and Lonely People* (Wheaton: Tyndale, 1972) 24-30.

4 Laurence J. Peter, *Peter's Quotations: Ideas for Our Time* (New York: Bantam, 1989) 417.

Chapter 4 – Sidestepping the People-Pleasing Trap

1   Billy and Janice Hughey, *A Rainbow of Hope: 777 Inspirational Quotes Plus Selected Stories* (El Reno: Rainbow Studies, 1994) 226.

2   W.H. Gispen. *Bible Student's Commentary: Exodus* (Grand Rapids: Zondervan, 1982) 292-93.

3   R. Alan Cole, *Exodus: An Introduction and Commentary* (Downers Grove: Inter-Varsity Press, 1974) 213-14.

4   Kenneth L. Barker and John Kohlenberger III, *Zondervan NIV Bible Commentary, Volume 1: Old Testament* (Grand Rapids: Zondervan, 1994) 119.

5   Harriet B. Braiker, *The Disease to Please: Curing the People-Pleasing Syndrome* (New York: McGraw-Hill, 2001) 161.

6   James W. Moore, *Some Folks Feel the Rain: Others Just Get Wet* (Nashville: Dimensions for Living, 1999) 115.

7   Braiker 66, 129-30.

8   Braiker 17, 181-82, 212.

9   William Barclay, *The Gospel of John, Volume 2* (Philadelphia: Westminster Press, 1975) 133.

Chapter 5 – Avoiding Games of Deceit

1   John H. Walton, Victor H. Matthews, and Mark W. Chavalas, *The IVP Bible Background Commentary: Old Testament* (Downers Grove: InterVarsity Press, 2000) 69-71.

Chapter 6 – Rattling Skeletons in Your Closet

1   Michael Mask, et al., *Family Secrets* (Nashville: Thomas Nelson, 1995) 10, 20-37, 44, 108-09.

2   John T. Willis, *Genesis* (Abilene: ACU Press, 1984) 344.

Chapter 7 – Making Hospitality Personal

1   Karen Mains, *Open Heart, Open Home* (Elgin: Cook, 1976) 26.

2   George Guthrie, "Hebrews," *Zondervan Illustrated Bible Backgrounds Commentary* (Grand Rapids: Zondervan, 2002) 79.

3   Neil R. Lightfoot, *Jesus Christ Today* (Abilene: Bible Guides, 1989) 246.

4   Murdock 103-04.

Chapter 8 – Discovering the Real Audience

1 William Barclay, *The Gospel of Luke*, rev. ed. (Louisville: Westminster John Knox Press, 2001) 265.

2 Walter Duckat, *Beggar to King: All the Occupations of Biblical Times* (Garden City: Doubleday, 1968) 254.

3 Lawrence O. Richards, Richards Complete Bible Dictionary (Iowa Falls: World Bible Publishers, 2002) 963.

Chapter 9 – Giving From the Heart

1 William Barclay, *The Gospel of Mark* (Philadelphia: Westminster Press, 1975) 302.

2 Michael J. Wilkins, "Matthew," *Zondervan Illustrated Bible Backgrounds Commentary, Volume 1: Matthew, Mark, Luke* (Grand Rapids: Zondervan, 2002) 44.

3 R. Alan Cole, *The Gospel According to Mark (The Tyndale New Testament Commentaries)* (Grand Rapids: Eerdmans, 1989) 271.

4 "Developing a Giving Heart," Bible.org, 15 March 2013 <http://bible.org/seriespage/developing-giving-heart>.

5 "Developing a Giving Heart."

6 D.E. Holwerda and Nola J. Opperwall-Galluch, "Widow," International Standard Bible Encyclopedia, Volume 3: Q-Z (Grand Rapids: Eerdmans, 1988) 1060-61.

7 Walton 70.

Chapter 10 – Breaking Up the Holy Huddle

1 Leon Morris, *The Gospel According to Luke (The Tyndale New Testament Commentaries)* (Grand Rapids: Eerdmans, 1988) 297.

2 Barclay, *Luke* 277.

3 Keener 240.

4 Stafford North, *Evangelizing Your Community* (Nashville: 21st Century Christian, 2007) 91.

5 Jay Pathak and David Runyon, *The Art of Neighboring: Building Genuine Relationships Right Outside the Door* (Grand Rapids: Baker Books, 2012) 144, 152-54.

6 North 89-90.

7 Thom S. Rainer, *The Unchurched Next Door: Understanding Faith Stages as Keys to Sharing Your Faith* (Grand Rapids: Zondervan, 2003) 167, 170-71.

8 North 91-93.

9 Rainer 73.

10 Bruce 59-60.

Chapter 11 – Saying What You Mean

1 Richard B. Wilke, *Tell Me Again, I'm Listening* (Nashville: Abingdon, 1973) 27.

2 Qtd. in Carmen Renee Berry and Tamara Traeder, *Girlfriends: Invisible Bonds, Enduring Ties* (Berkeley: Wildcat Canyon Press, 1995) 15.

3 John Powell, *Why Am I Afraid to Tell You Who I Am? Insights Into Personal Growth* (Allen: Argus Communications, 1969) 54-62.

4 Powell 74-75.

5 "Mind/Body Connection: How Your Emotions Affect Your Health," FamilyDoctor.org 20 April 2013 <http://familydoctor.org/familydoctor/en/prevention-wellness/emotional-wellbeing/mental-health/mind-body-connection-how-your-emotions-affect-your-health.html>.

6 Clinton McLemore, *Toxic Relationships and How to Change Them: Health and Holiness in Everyday Life* (San Francisco: Jossey-Bass, 2003) 11.

7 Brenda Waggoner, *The Velveteen Woman: Becoming Real Through God's Transforming Love* (Colorado Springs: Chariot Victor, 1999) 18-19.

8 Hughey 103.

Chapter 12 – Bursting Inflated Pride

1 Hughey 91.

2 Walton 736.

3 Herbert V. Prochnow, *The Speaker's Handbook of Epigrams and Witticisms* (New York: Harper and Row, 1955) 54.

4 Hughey 90.

Chapter 13 – Finding Your Ultimate Security

1 Julianna Slattery, *Beyond the Masquerade: Unveiling the Authentic You* (Carol Stream: Tyndale House, 2007) 49, 75.

2 Slattery 50-54, 58.

3 Qtd. in Slattery 133.

4 Slattery 63-65, 99.

CPSIA information can be obtained at www.ICGtesting.com
Printed in the USA
LVOW10s1756141213

365327LV00002B/2/P